Music Moves for Piano

Keyalities and Tonalities

The Complete Book of Arpeggios, Cadences and Scales

By Marilyn Lowe
In cooperation with Edwin E. Gordon

Music Moves for Piano is designed to develop improvisation, audiation and keyboard performance skills. The piano series builds on the ideas and theories of Orff, Kodaly, Dalcroze, Suzuki, Taubman and Gordon.

G-7056

www.musicmovesforpiano.com
info@musicmovesforpiano.com
ISBN-10: 1-57999-634-5

Distributed by GIA Publications, Inc.
7404 S. Mason Ave., Chicago, IL 60638
(708) 496-3800 or (800) 442-1358
www.giamusic.com

Printed in the United States of America.

Table of Contents

Unit 13 - Other Tonalities

Appendix

Suggestions For Using This Book

Introduction

The purpose of this book is to help the keyboard player acquire an aural and kinesthetic knowledge of all the keyalities and tonalities. This knowledge is the foundation for successful reading, improvisation and performance. Keyalities and Tonalities may be used as a reference book, to introduce new students to tonal solfege, to learn the sounds and cadences for eight different tonalities, and for review projects.

The keyalities in this book are arranged in the circle of 4ths, also known as the circle of dominants. Each keyality is the dominant of the next keyality. Letter names of the tonic, such as A or E, are keyalities.

The tonalities are arranged alphabetically: Aeolian, Dorian, Harmonic Minor, Lydian, Locrian, Major, Mixolydian, and Phrygian. Each tonality has its own resting tone/tonic, such as DO (Major), LA (Harmonic Minor and Aeolian), RE (Dorian), and so forth.

The sharps or flats that denote the letter name of DO (traditionally called a key signature) is a DO signature. One DO signature represents all the tonalities. For example, when F is DO (Major tonality), then D is LA (Harmonic Minor tonality or Aeolian tonality), G is RE (Dorian tonality), C is SO (Mixolydian tonality), and so forth. The syllable name for a tonality is the resting tone.The 'moveable DO with a LA-based Minor solfege system' is the only solfege system that fosters audiation.

Study Ideas

1. Have students use this book as a reference for transposing.
2. Establish a project of "unit study" for several weeks, during which time students emphasize one DO signature. Study scales, arpeggios and cadences in different tonalities; learn performance pieces; improvise,transpose, compose and create arrangements.
3. Introduce a new tonality, such as Dorian or Phrygian, during the study of any Major keyality if the student demonstrates interest. These tonalities are presented in Unit 13.
4. Establish a "unit study" to practice all the tonalities one DO signature represents. Master the cadences, improvise, transpose, compose and create arrangements. Students should sing the syllables of the primary triads for each tonality.
5. Use this book to introduce tonal solfege to transfer students. Have students sing the syllables for the primary triads of each tonality. Before playing arpeggioed cadences, have students sing the roots of each triad in order to hear and reinfore the root harmony. Then have students learn where the root chord changes are located on the keyboard for each keyality and tonality . This aural and kinesthetic knowledge provides a basic foundation for improvisation, arranging, and composing as well as for reading and writing music fluently.
6. Teachers and students may create a variety of improvisation activities for each keyality and tonality. For example, have students improvise a melody using the following: one phrase (four DUs) using tones from the tonic triad, one phrase using tones from the dominant triad, one phrase using tones from the tonic triad, and the final phrase using tones from the dominant triad then the tonic triad. At first, use the root chord changes for the accompaniment. Other suggestions are:
   - Have students play folk songs in different tonalities.
   - Have students improvise a two-four phrase melody in different tonalties that have the same DO signature OR tonic.
7. Challenge students to learn to play the Major and/or Harmonic Minor scales two, three and four octaves with the metronome. The Harmonic Minor scale is presented on page 81. Keep a metronome chart to encourage students to increase speed.
8. Remind students that they are storing permanent files in the brain, similar to computer files, for quick access to every keyality and tonality. This information is useful in performance, for learning new music with or without notation, and for creative activities such as improvising, arranging and composing.

Unit 1

Check List

Tonic Arpeggio

Lesson		Home
________	Separated	________
________	Connected	________
________	Sing Syllables	________

Melodic Cadence

Lesson		Home
________	Hand	________
________	Hand	________
________	Separated	________
________	Connected	________
________	Sing Syllables	________
________	Add LH Roots	________

Transposition

Lesson		Home
________	Folk Song	________
________	Folk Song	________
________	Solo	________
________	Solo	________

Major Tonality - When DO is C

Tonic Arpeggio

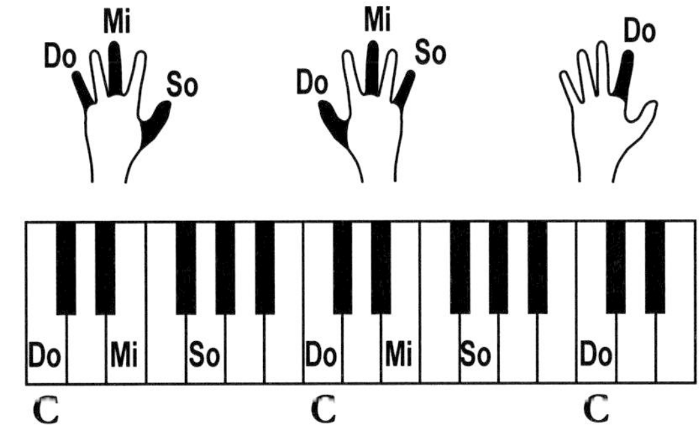

This picture is the keyboard "look" and "feel" of a C Major arpeggio: W W W

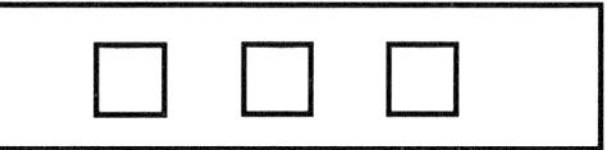

Tonic-Dominant-Tonic Melodic Cadence

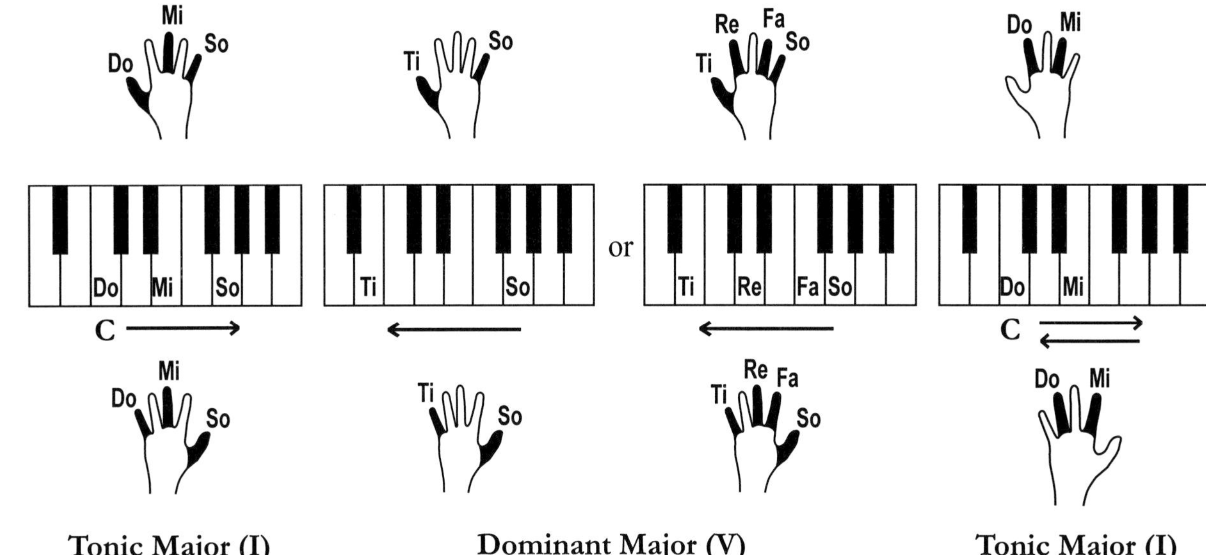

C Major Scale

DO is C

Play the scale with one finger.

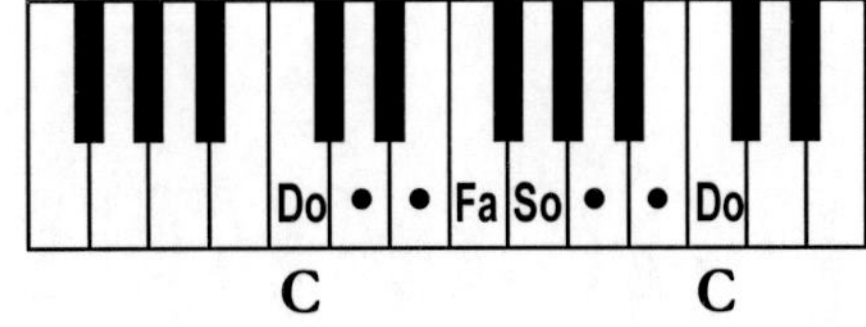

This picture is the keyboard "look" and "feel" of a C Major scale. All the keys are white.

Check List

Major Scale

Lesson		Home
________	Hand	________
________	Hand	________
________	Separated	________
________	Connected	________
________	One Octave	________
________	Two Octaves	________
________	Three Octaves	________
________	Four Octaves	________

Learn the thumb crossings.

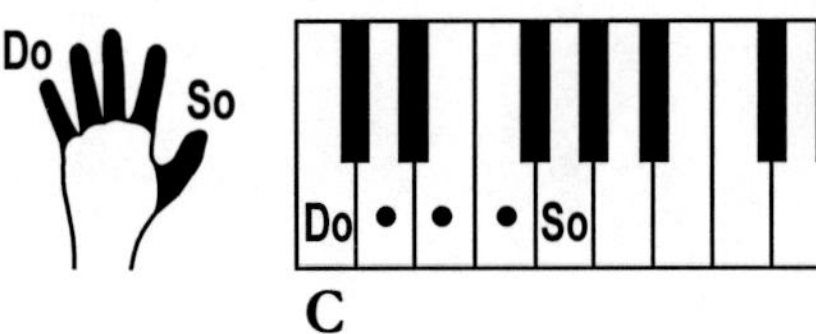

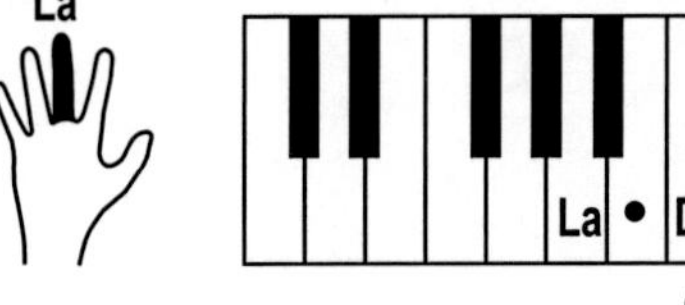

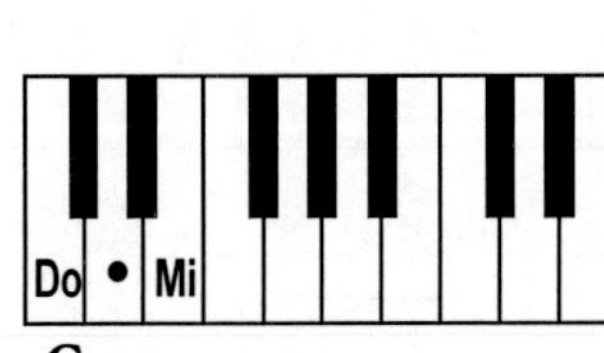

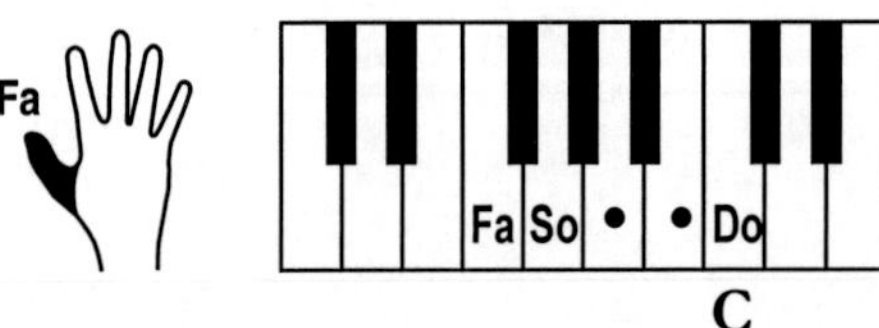

Play the scale from DO to DO.

Harmonic Minor Tonality - When LA is A

Check List

Tonic Arpeggio

Lesson		Home
________	Separated	________
________	Connected	________
________	Sing Syllables	________

Melodic Cadence

Lesson		Home
________	Hand	________
________	Hand	________
________	Separated	________
________	Connected	________
________	Sing Syllables	________
________	Add LH Roots	________

Transposition

Lesson		Home
________	Folk Song	________
________	Folk Song	________
________	Solo	________
________	Solo	________

Tonic Arpeggio

This picture is the keyboard "look" and "feel" of an A Minor arpeggio: W W W

Tonic-Dominant-Tonic Melodic Cadence

(Alternate fingering for RH is on page 9)

Tonic Minor (i) — Dominant Harmonic Minor (V) — Tonic Minor (i)

Tonic - Dominant - Tonic Arpeggios
When DO is C then LA is A

Check List

Major Tonality

Lesson		Home
________	Separated	________
________	Connected	________
________	Sing Syllables	________

Harmonic Minor Tonality

Lesson		Home
________	Separated	________
________	Connected	________
________	Sing Syllables	________

When DO is C then LA is A

La Do Mi So
A C

Fingers to Use

Tonic-Dominant-Tonic Arpeggios

DO is C

Do Mi So
C
Tonic Major (I)

So Ti Re
Dominant Major (V)

Do Mi So
C
Tonic Major (I)

LA is A

La Do Mi
A
Tonic Minor (i)

Mi Si Ti
Dominant Harmonic Minor (V)

La Do Mi
A
Tonic Minor (i)

Tonic - Subdominant - Tonic
When DO is C

Check List

Melodic Cadence

Lesson		Home
________	Hand	________
________	Hand	________
________	Separated	________
________	Connected	________
________	Sing Syllables	________
________	Play I-IV-V-I	________
________	Add LH Roots	________

Arpeggios

Lesson		Home
________	Separated	________
________	Connected	________
________	Sing Syllables	________
________	Play I-IV-V-I	________

Melodic Cadence

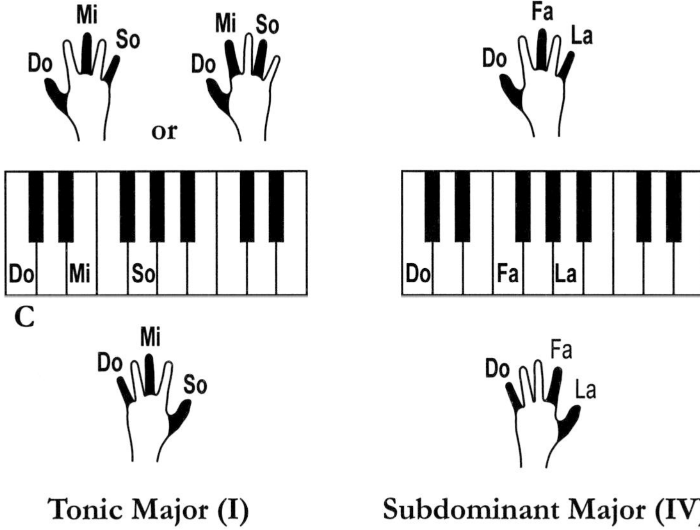

Tonic Major (I)

Subdominant Major (IV)

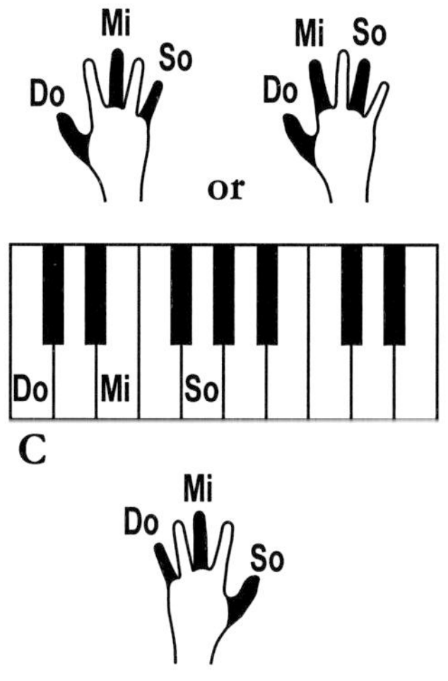

Tonic Major (I)

Arpeggios

Fingers to Use

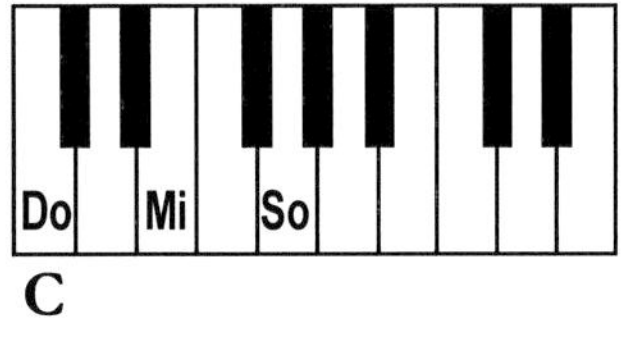

Tonic Major (I)

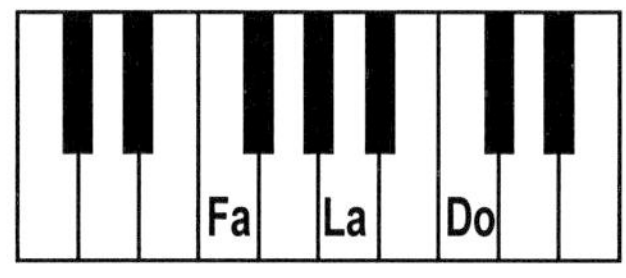

Subdominant Major (IV)

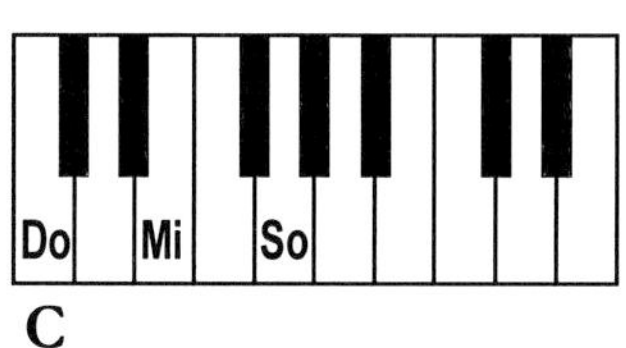

Tonic Major (I)

Tonic - Subdominant - Tonic
When LA is A

Check List

Melodic Cadence

Lesson		Home
________	Hand	________
________	Hand	________
________	Separated	________
________	Connected	________
________	Sing Syllables	________
________	Play i-iv-V-i	________
________	Add LH Roots	________

Arpeggios

Lesson		Home
________	Separated	________
________	Connected	________
________	Sing Syllables	________
________	Play i-iv-V-i	________

Melodic Cadence

Tonic Minor (i) Subdominant Minor (iv) Tonic Minor (i)

Arpeggios

Fingers to Use

Tonic Minor (i) Subdominant Minor (iv) Tonic Minor (i)

Check List

Tonic Arpeggio

Lesson		Home
________	Separated	________
________	Connected	________
________	Sing Syllables	________

Melodic Cadence

Lesson		Home
________	Hand	________
________	Hand	________
________	Separated	________
________	Connected	________
________	Sing Syllables	________
________	Add LH Roots	________

Transposition

Lesson		Home
________	Folk Song	________
________	Folk Song	________
________	Solo	________
________	Solo	________

Major Tonality - When DO is F

Tonic Arpeggio

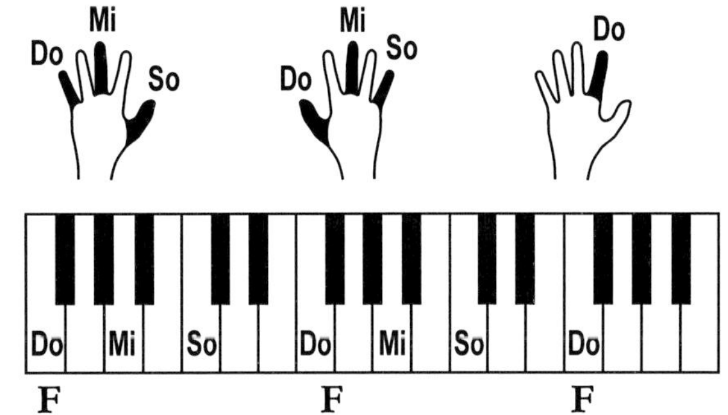

This picture is the keyboard "look" and "feel" of an F Major arpeggio: W W W

Tonic-Dominant-Tonic Melodic Cadence

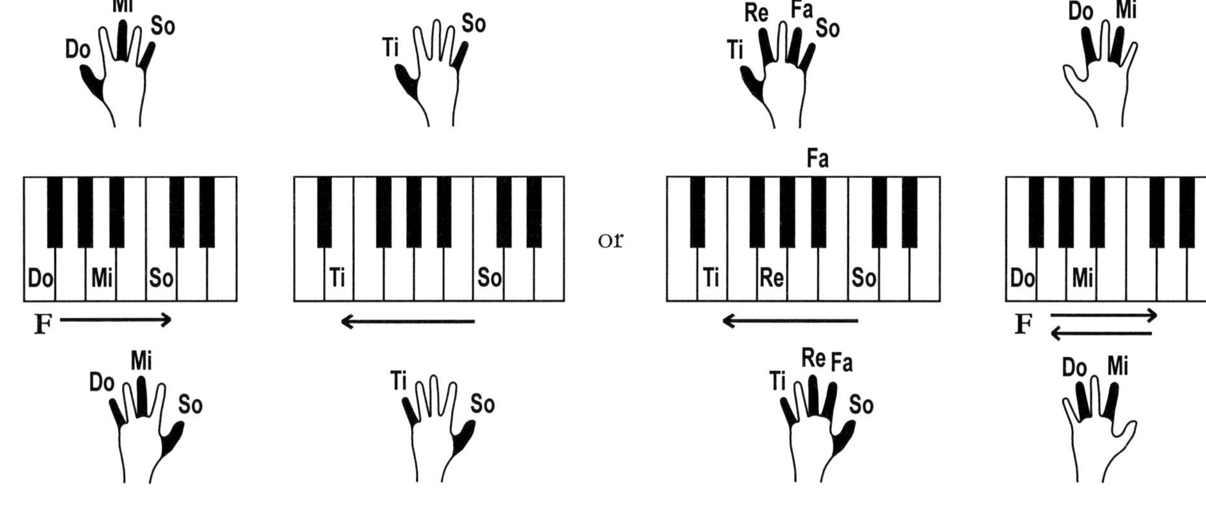

Tonic Major (I) Dominant Major (V) Tonic Major (I)

F Major Scale

DO is F

Play the scale with one finger.

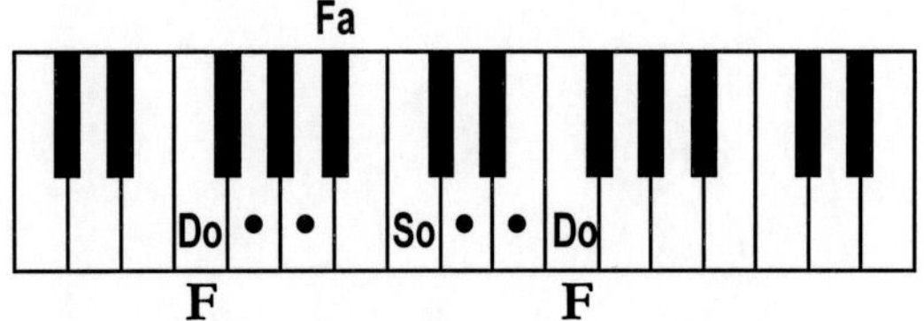

This picture is the keyboard "look" and "feel" of an F Major scale. There is one black key.

Check List

Major Scale

Lesson		Home
________	Hand	________
________	Hand	________
________	Separated	________
________	Connected	________
________	One Octave	________
________	Two Octaves	________
________	Three Octaves	________
________	Four Octaves	________

Learn the thumb crossings.

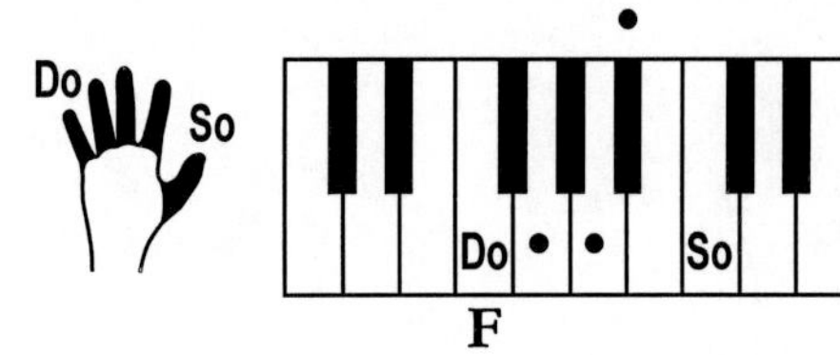

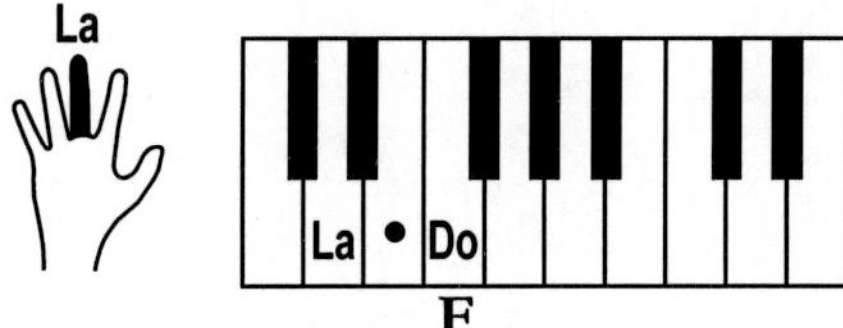

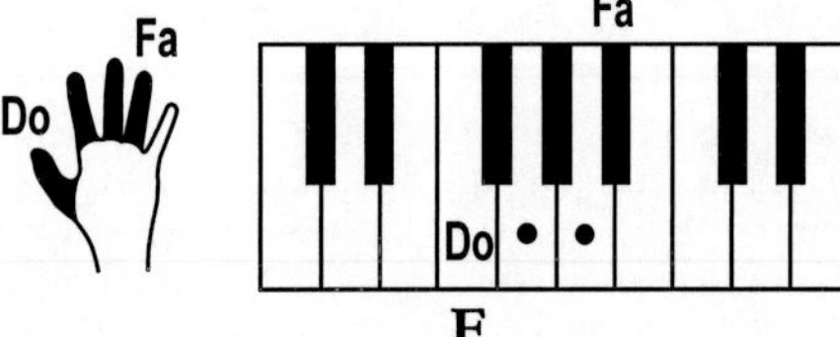

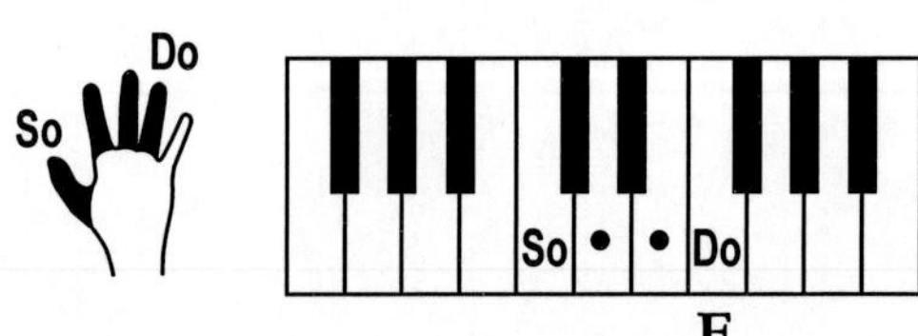

Play the scale from DO to DO.

Harmonic Minor Tonality - When LA is D

Check List

Tonic Arpeggio

Lesson		Home
________	Separated	________
________	Connected	________
________	Sing Syllables	________

Melodic Cadence

Lesson		Home
________	Hand	________
________	Hand	________
________	Separated	________
________	Connected	________
________	Sing Syllables	________
________	Add LH Roots	________

Transposition

Lesson		Home
________	Folk Song	________
________	Folk Song	________
________	Solo	________
________	Solo	________

Tonic Arpeggio

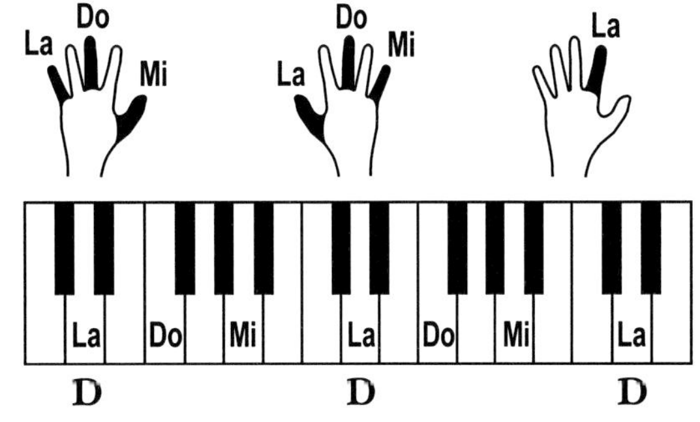

This picture is the keyboard "look" and "feel" of a D Minor arpeggio: W W W

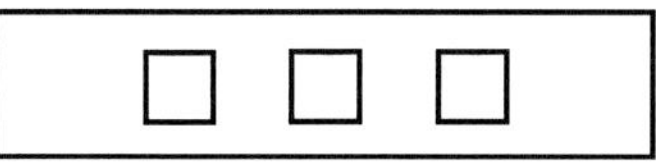

Tonic-Dominant-Tonic Melodic Cadence

(Alternate fingering for RH is on page 3)

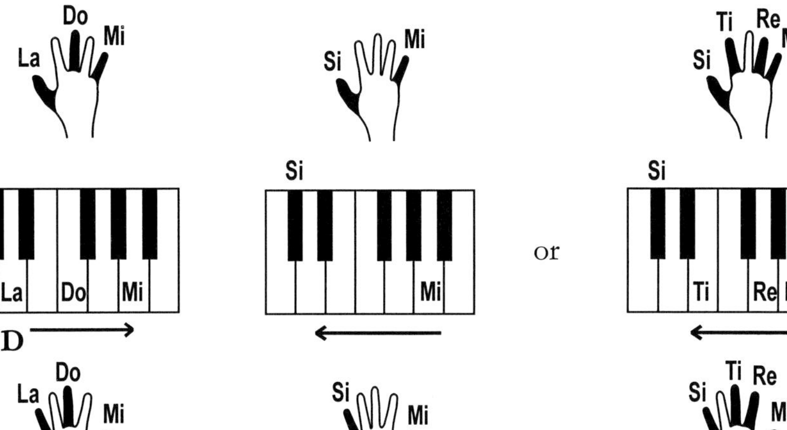

Tonic Minor (i) Dominant Harmonic Minor (V) Tonic Minor (i)

Tonic - Dominant - Tonic Arpeggios
When DO is F then LA is D

Check List

Major Tonality

Lesson		Home
________	Separated	________
________	Connected	________
________	Sing Syllables	________

Harmonic Minor Tonality

Lesson		Home
________	Separated	________
________	Connected	________
________	Sing Syllables	________

When DO is F then LA is D

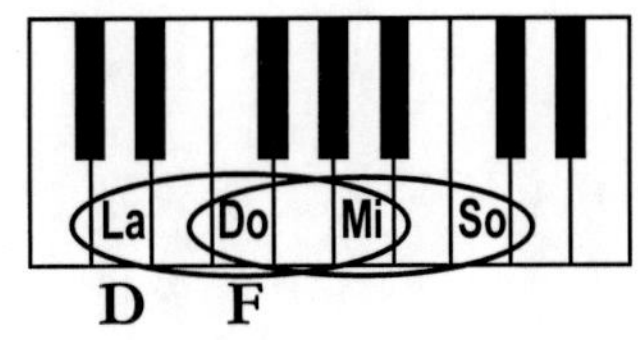

Fingers to Use

Tonic-Dominant-Tonic Arpeggios

DO is F

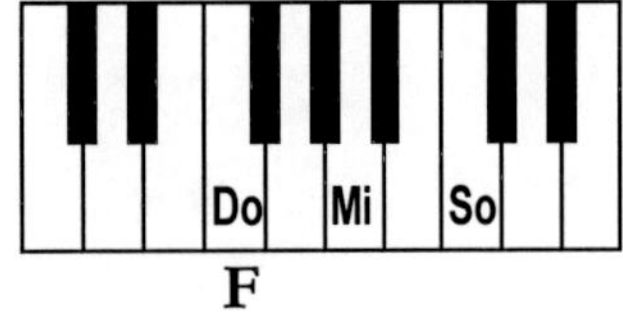

Tonic Major (I)

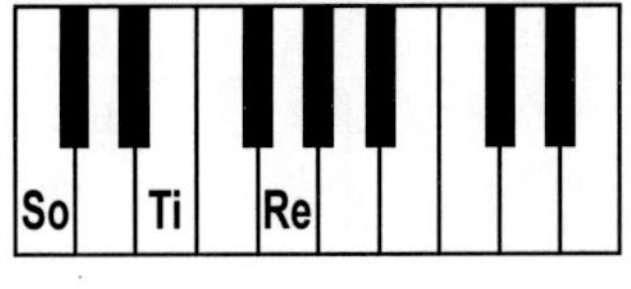

Dominant Major (V)

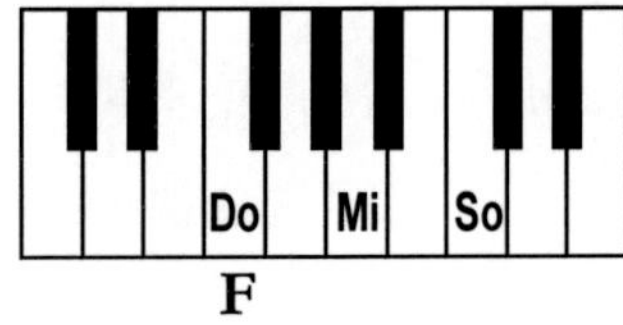

Tonic Major (I)

LA is D

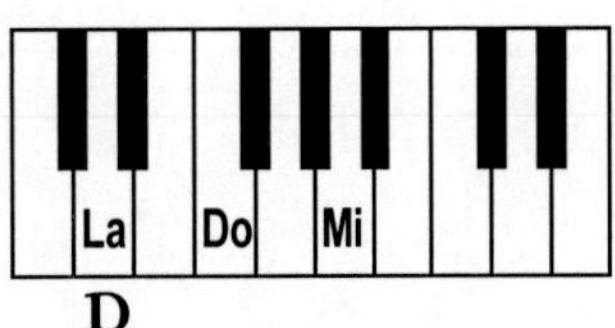

Tonic Minor (i)

Si

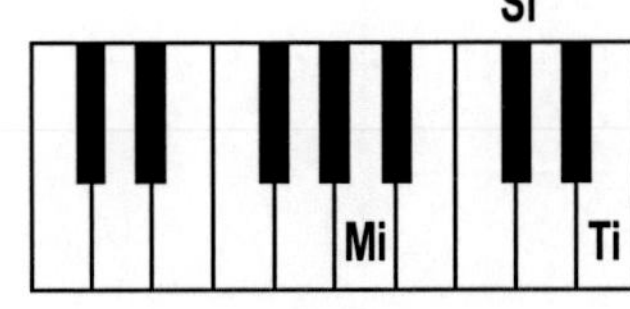

Dominant Harmonic Minor (V)

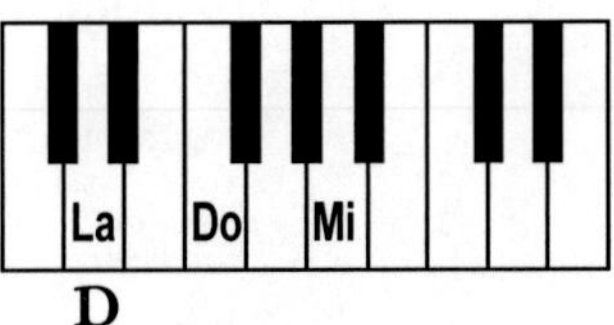

Tonic Minor (i)

Tonic - Subdominant - Tonic
When DO is F

Check List

Melodic Cadence

Lesson		Home
______	Hand	______
______	Hand	______
______	Separated	______
______	Connected	______
______	Sing Syllables	______
______	Play I-IV-V-I	______
______	Add LH Roots	______

Arpeggios

Lesson		Home
______	Separated	______
______	Connected	______
______	Sing Syllables	______
______	Play I-IV-V-I	______

Melodic Cadence

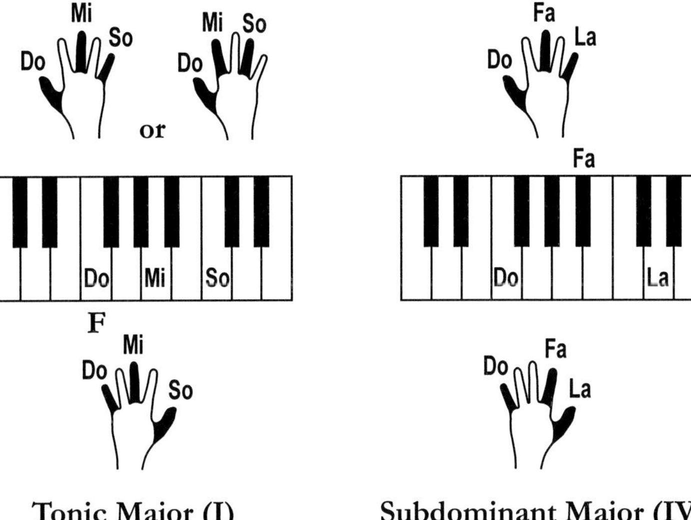

Tonic Major (I)

Subdominant Major (IV)

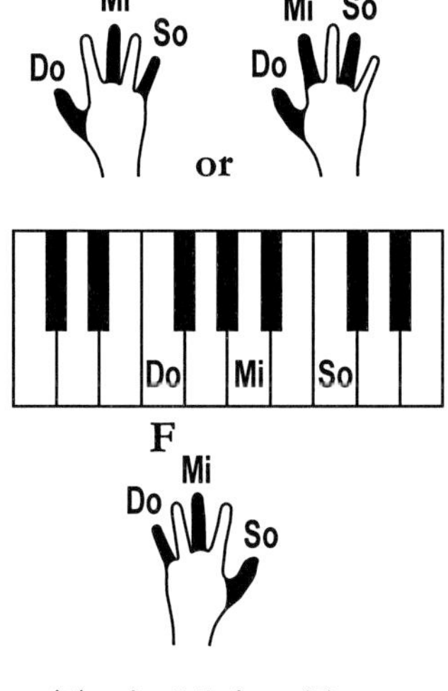

Tonic Major (I)

Arpeggios

Fingers to Use

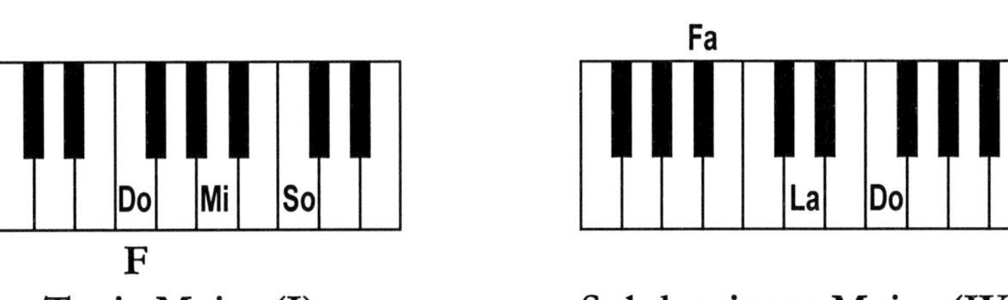

F

Tonic Major (I)

Subdominant Major (IV)

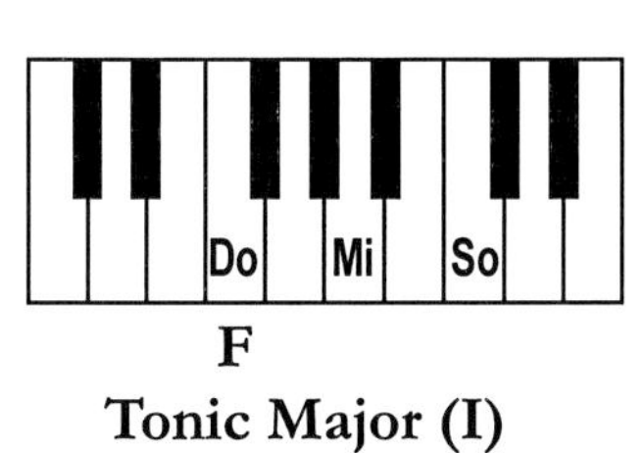

F

Tonic Major (I)

Tonic - Subdominant - Tonic
When LA is D

Check List

Melodic Cadence

Lesson		Home
________	Hand	________
________	Hand	________
________	Separated	________
________	Connected	________
________	Sing Syllables	________
________	Play i-iv-V-i	________
________	Add LH Roots	________

Arpeggios

Lesson		Home
________	Separated	________
________	Connected	________
________	Sing Syllables	________
________	Play i-iv-V-i	________

Melodic Cadence

La Do Mi or La Do Mi

La Do Mi

D

La Do Mi

Tonic Minor (i)

La Re Fa

Fa

La Re

La Re Fa

Subdominant Minor (iv)

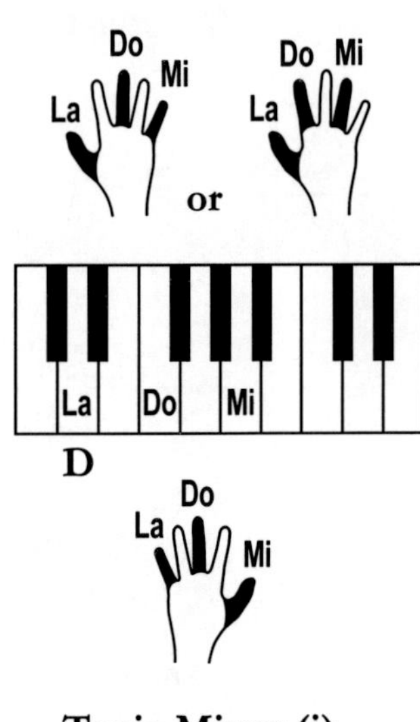

Tonic Minor (i)

Arpeggios

La Do Mi

D

Tonic Minor (i)

Fingers to Use

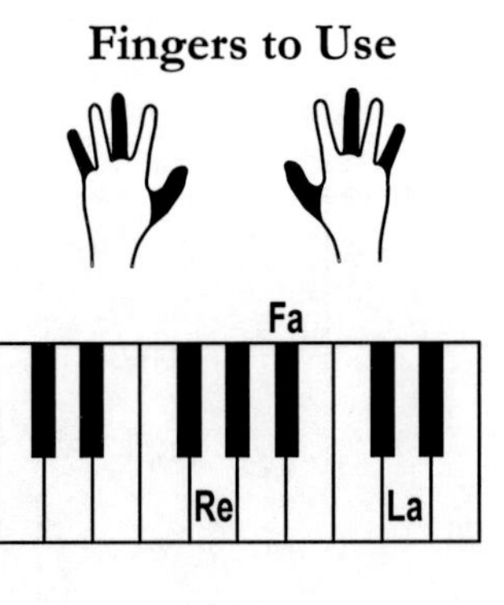

Subdominant Minor (iv)

Tonic Minor (i)

Check List

Tonic Arpeggio

Lesson		Home
________	Separated	________
________	Connected	________
________	Sing Syllables	________

Melodic Cadence

Lesson		Home
________	Hand	________
________	Hand	________
________	Separated	________
________	Connected	________
________	Sing Syllables	________
________	Add LH Roots	________

Transposition

Lesson		Home
________	Folk Song	________
________	Folk Song	________
________	Solo	________
________	Solo	________

Major Tonality – When DO is B♭

Tonic Arpeggio

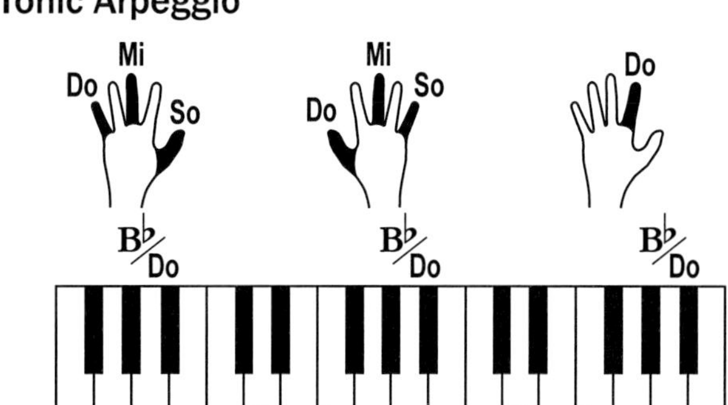

This picture is the keyboard "look" and "feel" of a B♭ Major arpeggio: B W W

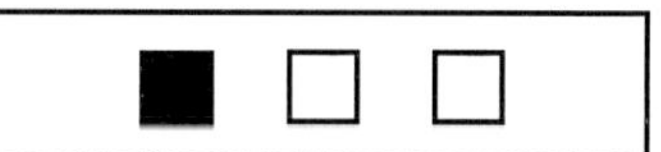

Tonic-Dominant-Tonic Melodic Cadence

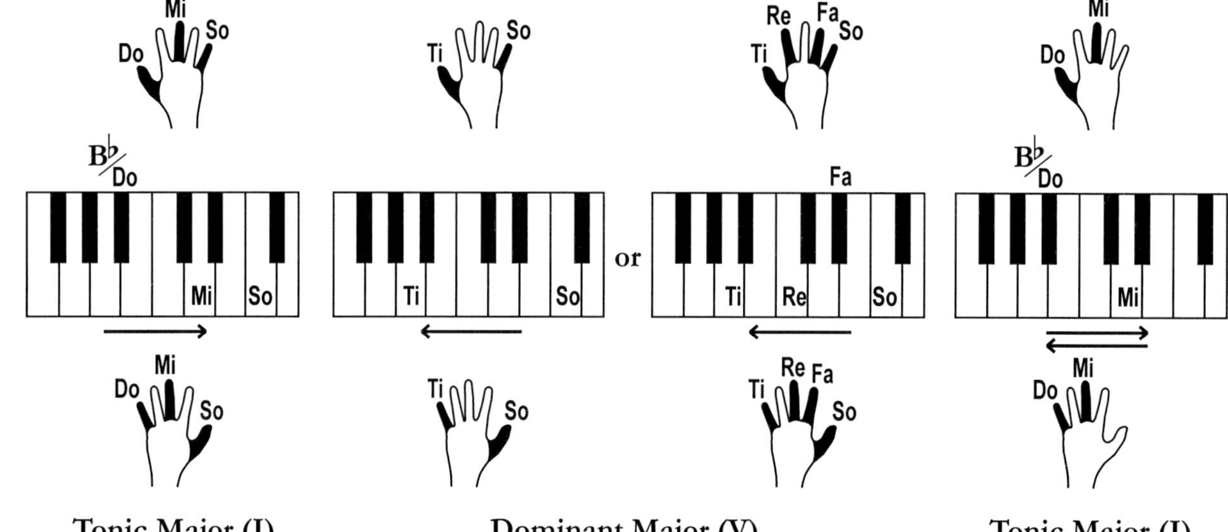

Tonic Major (I) Dominant Major (V) Tonic Major (I)

B♭ Major Scale

DO is B♭

Play the scale with one finger.

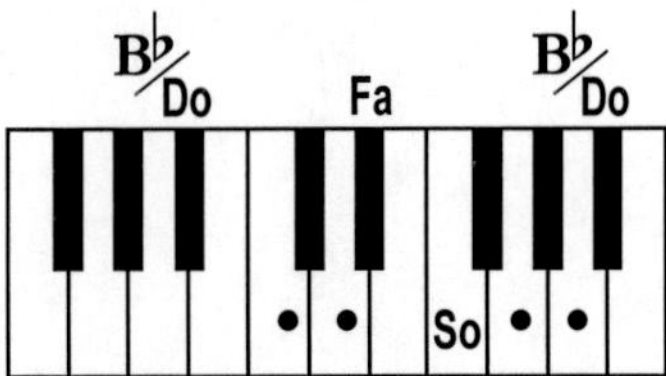

This picture is the keyboard "look" and "feel" of a B♭ Major scale:
B W W B W W W B

Check List

Major Scale

Lesson		Home
________	Hand	________
________	Hand	________
________	Separated	________
________	Connected	________
________	One Octave	________
________	Two Octaves	________
________	Three Octaves	________
________	Four Octaves	________

Learn the thumb crossings.

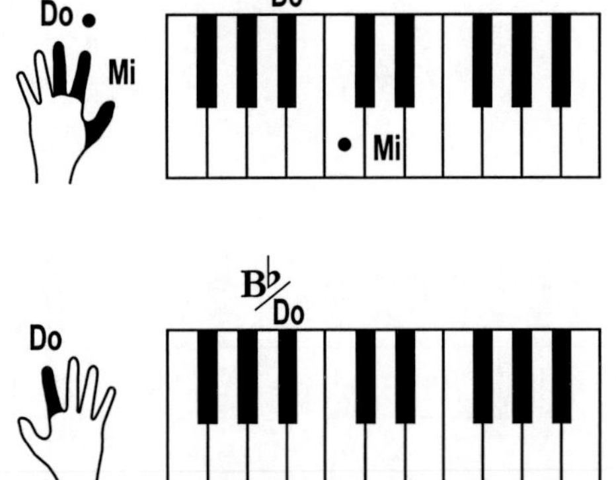

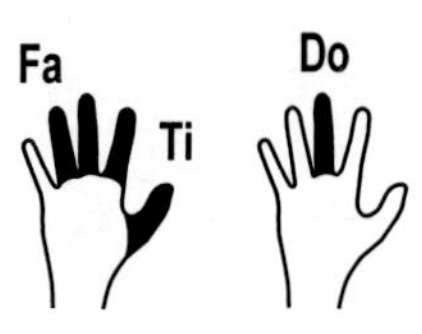

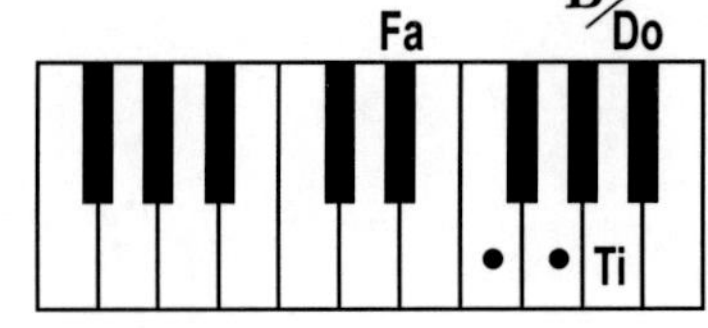

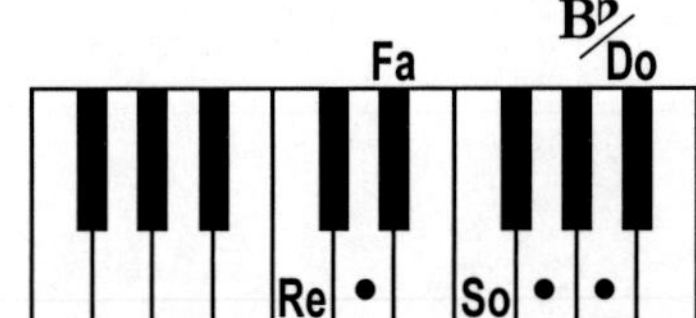

Play the scale from DO to DO.

Harmonic Minor Tonality – When LA is G

Check List

Tonic Arpeggio

Lesson		Home
________	Separated	________
________	Connected	________
________	Sing Syllables	________

Melodic Cadence

Lesson		Home
________	Hand	________
________	Hand	________
________	Separated	________
________	Connected	________
________	Sing Syllables	________
________	Add LH Roots	________

Transposition

Lesson		Home
________	Folk Song	________
________	Folk Song	________
________	Solo	________
________	Solo	________

Tonic Arpeggio

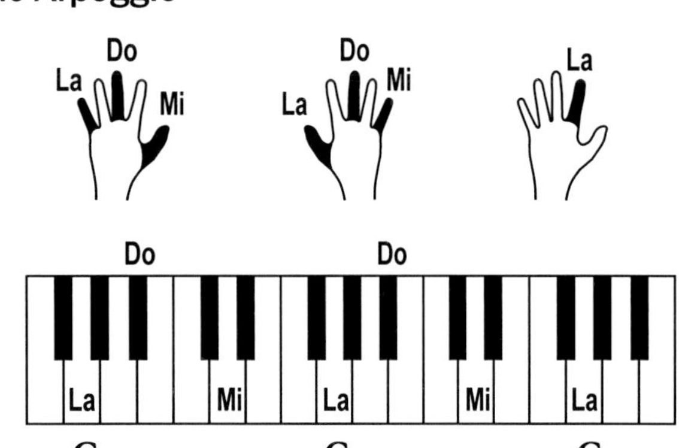

This picture is the keyboard "look" and "feel" of a G Minor arpeggio: W B W

Tonic-Dominant-Tonic Melodic Cadence

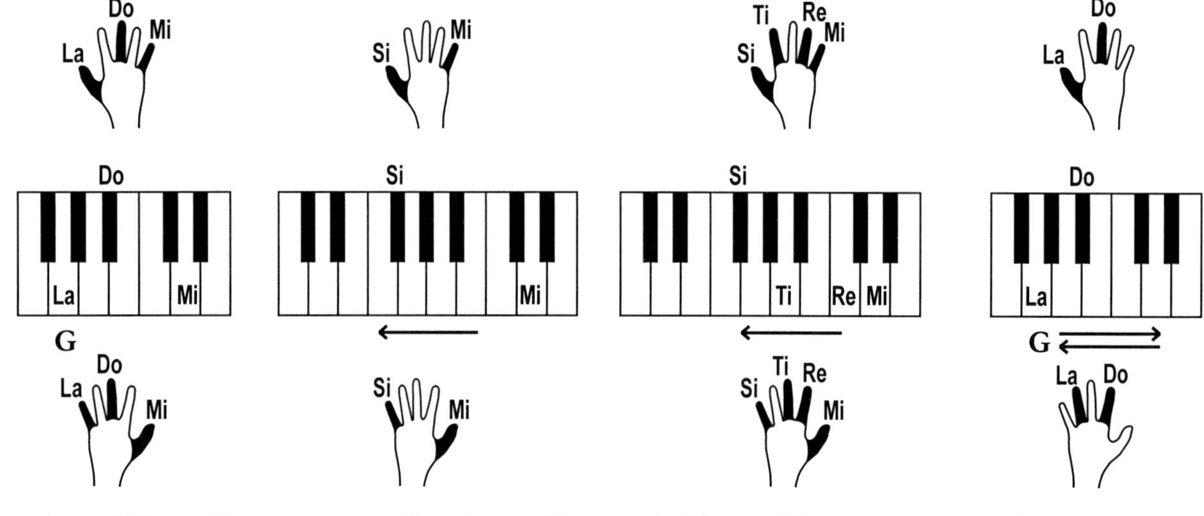

Tonic Minor (i) Dominant Harmonic Minor (V) Tonic Minor (i)

Tonic – Dominant - Tonic Arpeggios
When DO is B♭ then LA is G

Check List

Major Tonality

Lesson		Home
________	Separated	________
________	Connected	________
________	Sing Syllables	________

Harmonic Minor Tonality

Lesson		Home
________	Separated	________
________	Connected	________
________	Sing Syllables	________

When DO is B♭ then LA is G

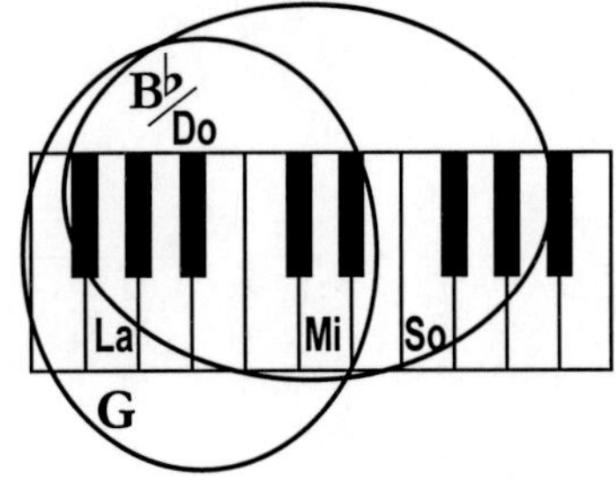

Fingers to Use

Tonic-Dominant-Tonic Arpeggios

Do is B♭

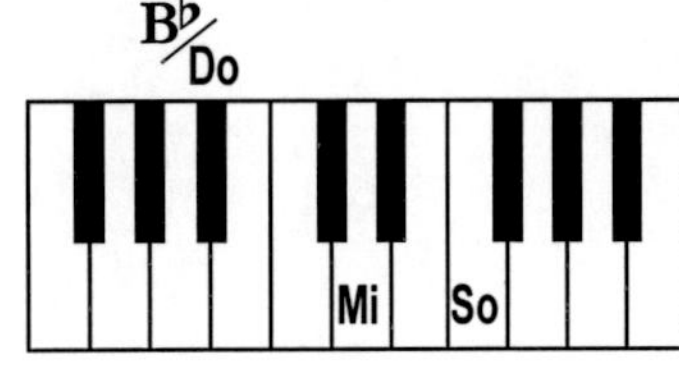

Tonic Major (I)

So Ti Re

Dominant Major (V)

B♭/Do

Mi So

Tonic Major (I)

LA is G

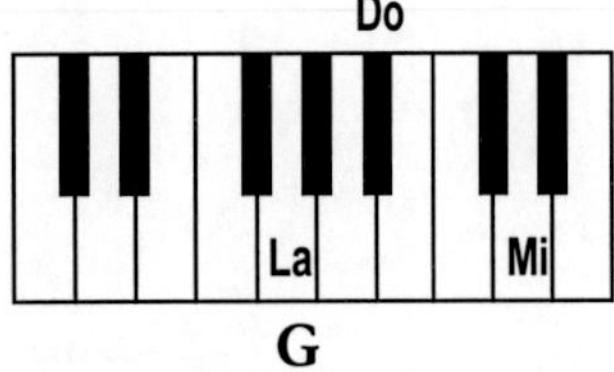

Tonic Minor (i)

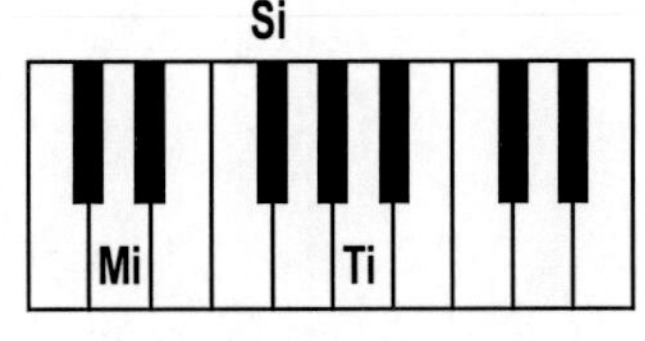

Dominant Harmonic Minor (V)

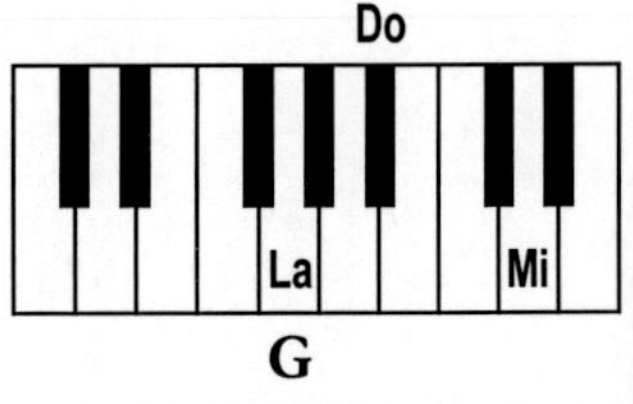

Tonic Minor (i)

Tonic – Subdominant - Tonic
When DO is B♭

Check List

Melodic Cadence

Lesson		Home
________	Hand	________
________	Hand	________
________	Separated	________
________	Connected	________
________	Sing Syllables	________
________	Play I-IV-V-I	________
________	Add LH Roots	________

Arpeggios

Lesson		Home
________	Separated	________
________	Connected	________
________	Sing Syllables	________
________	Play I-IV-V-I	________

Melodic Cadence

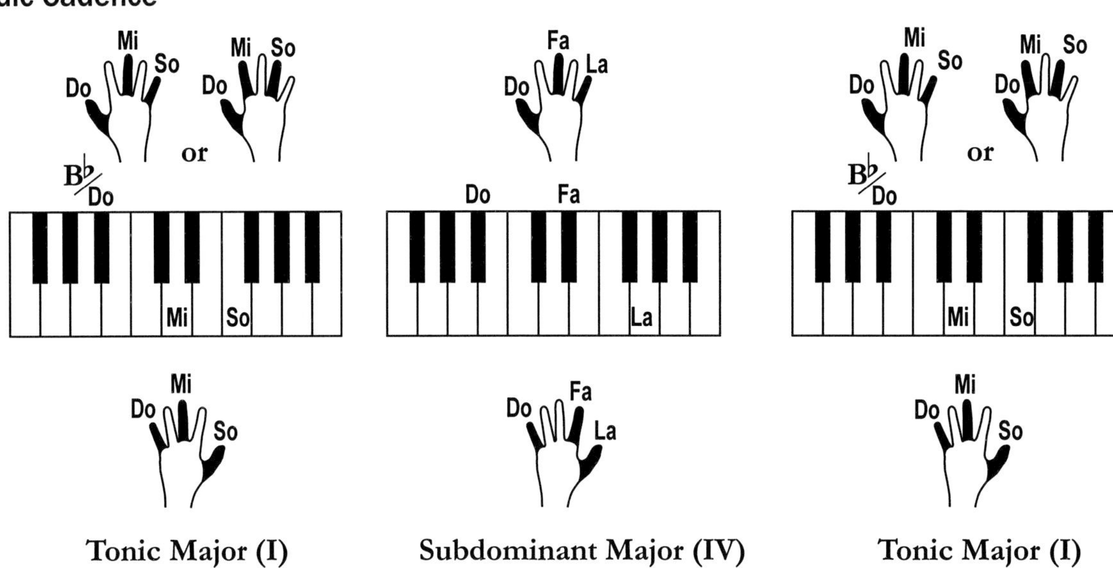

Tonic Major (I) — Subdominant Major (IV) — Tonic Major (I)

Arpeggios

Fingers to Use

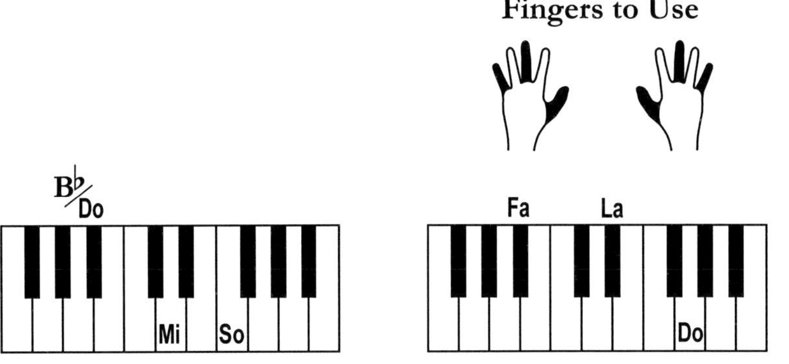

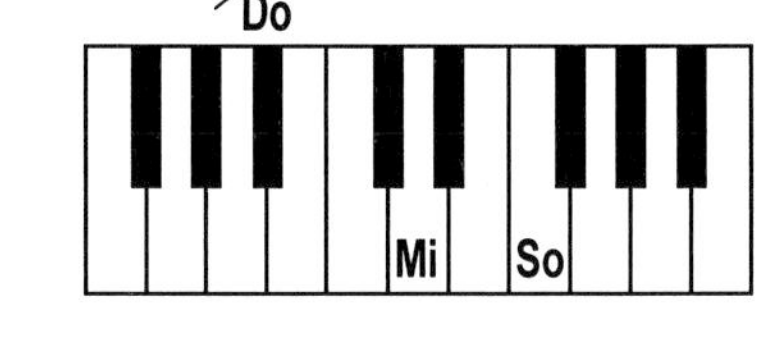

Tonic Major (I) — Subdominant Major (IV) — Tonic Major (I)

Tonic – Subdominant - Tonic
When LA is G

Check List

Melodic Cadence

Lesson		Home
________	Hand	________
________	Hand	________
________	Separated	________
________	Connected	________
________	Sing Syllables	________
________	Play i-iv-V-i	________
________	Add LH Roots	________

Arpeggios

Lesson		Home
________	Separated	________
________	Connected	________
________	Sing Syllables	________
________	Play i-iv-V-i	________

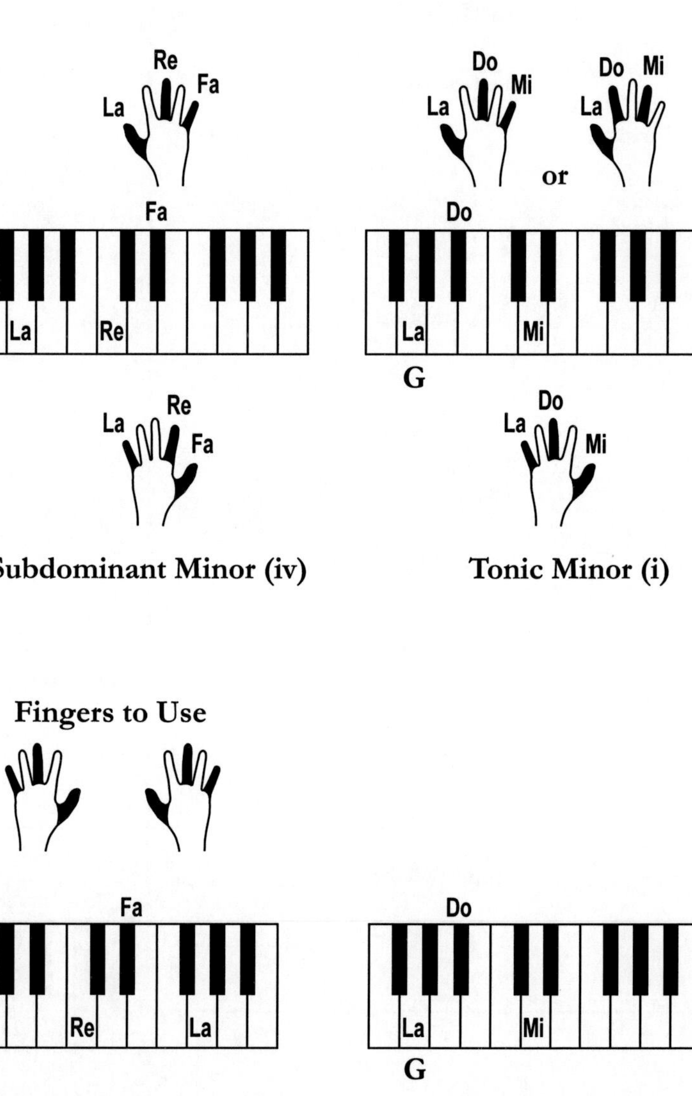

Unit 4

Major Tonality – When DO is E♭

Check List

Tonic Arpeggio

Lesson		Home
______	Separated	______
______	Connected	______
______	Sing Syllables	______

Melodic Cadence

Lesson		Home
______	Hand	______
______	Hand	______
______	Separated	______
______	Connected	______
______	Sing Syllables	______
______	Add LH Roots	______

Transposition

Lesson		Home
______	Folk Song	______
______	Folk Song	______
______	Solo	______
______	Solo	______

Tonic Arpeggio

Do Mi So
Do Mi So
Do
E♭/Do So E♭/Do So E♭/Do
Mi Mi

This picture is the keyboard "look" and "feel" of an E♭ Major arpeggio: B W B

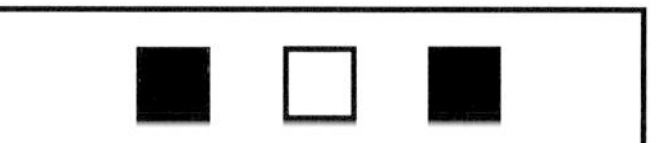

Tonic-Dominant-Tonic Melodic Cadence

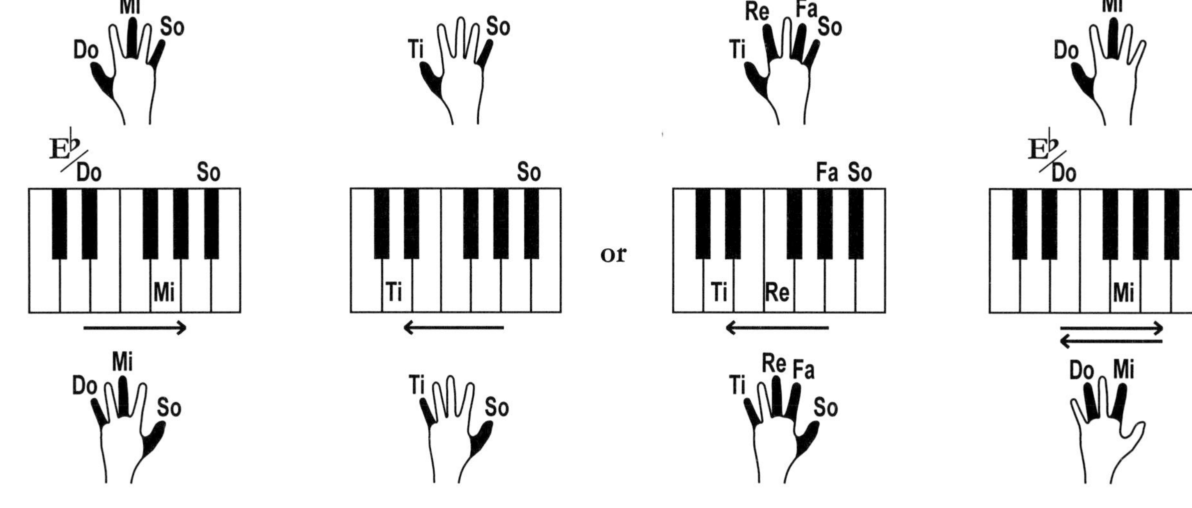

Tonic Major (I) Dominant Major (V) Tonic Major (I)

E♭ Major Scale

DO is E♭

Play the scale with one finger.

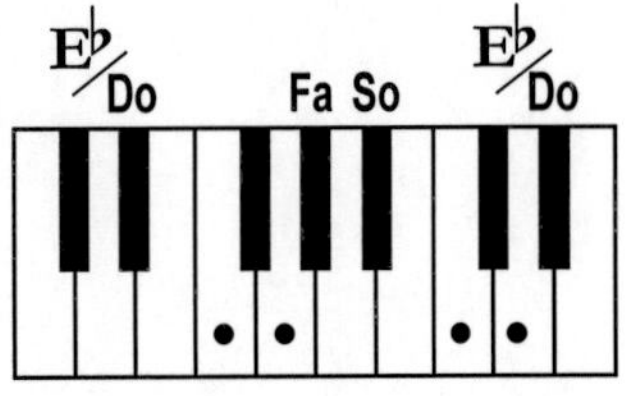

This picture is the keyboard "look" and "feel" of an E♭ Major scale:
B W W B B W W B

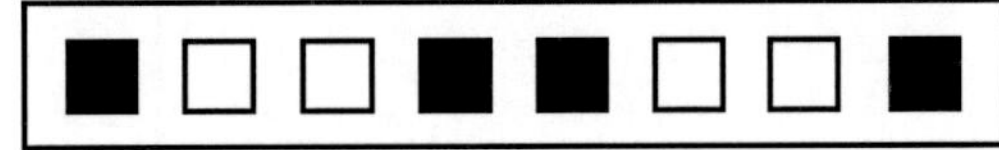

Check List

Major Scale

Lesson		Home
________	Hand	________
________	Hand	________
________	Separated	________
________	Connected	________
________	One Octave	________
________	Two Octaves	________
________	Three Octaves	________
________	Four Octaves	________

Learn the thumb crossings.

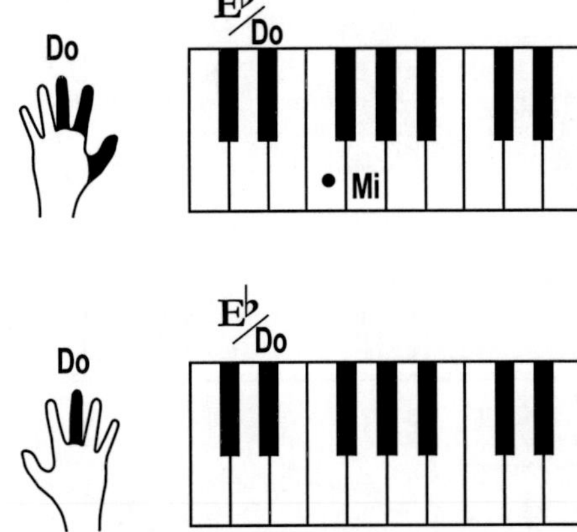

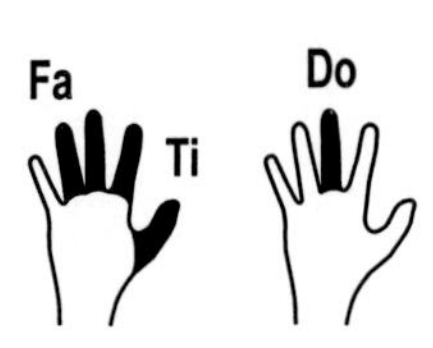

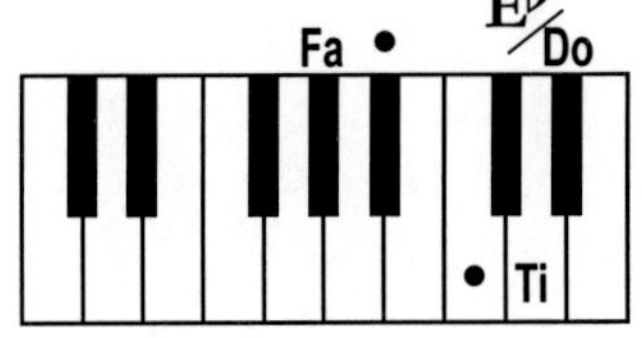

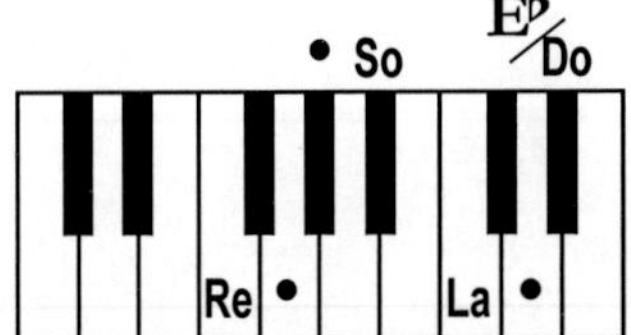

Play the scale from DO to DO.

Harmonic Minor Tonality – When LA is C

Check List

Tonic Arpeggio

Lesson		Home
________	Separated	________
________	Connected	________
________	Sing Syllables	________

Melodic Cadence

Lesson		Home
________	Hand	________
________	Hand	________
________	Separated	________
________	Connected	________
________	Sing Syllables	________
________	Add LH Roots	________

Transposition

Lesson		Home
________	Folk Song	________
________	Folk Song	________
________	Solo	________
________	Solo	________

Tonic Arpeggio

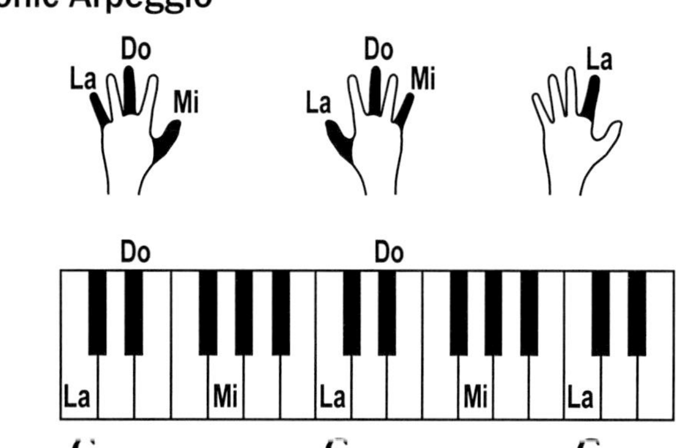

This picture is the keyboard "look" and "feel" of a C Minor arpeggio: W B W

Tonic-Dominant-Tonic Melodic Cadence

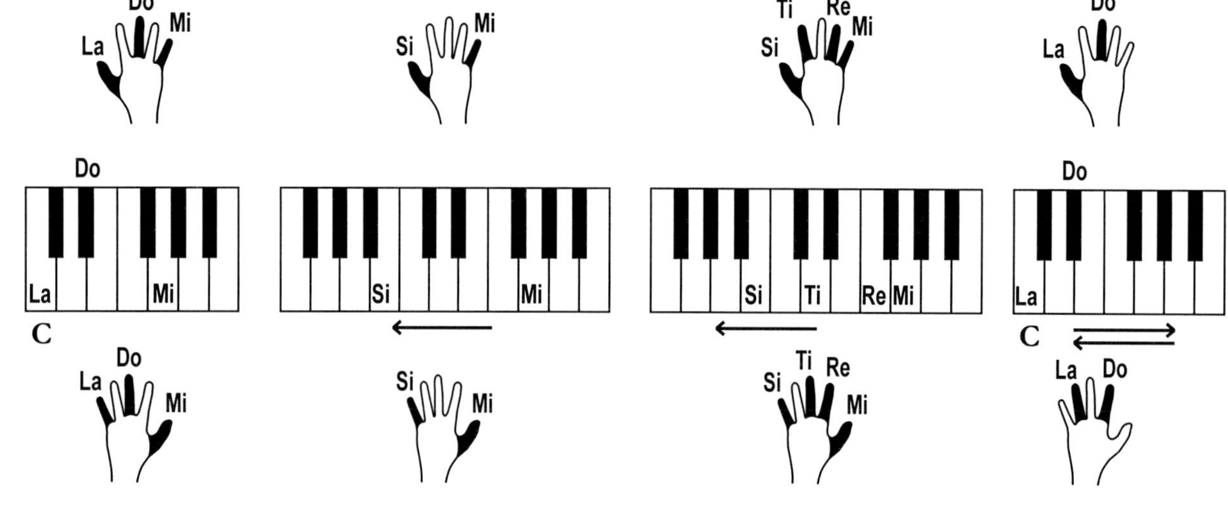

Tonic Minor (i) Dominant Harmonic Minor (V) Tonic Minor (i)

Tonic – Dominant - Tonic Arpeggios
When DO is E♭ then LA is C

Check List

Major Tonality

Lesson		Home
________	Separated	________
________	Connected	________
________	Sing Syllables	________

Harmonic Minor Tonality

Lesson		Home
________	Separated	________
________	Connected	________
________	Sing Syllables	________

When DO is E♭ then LA is C

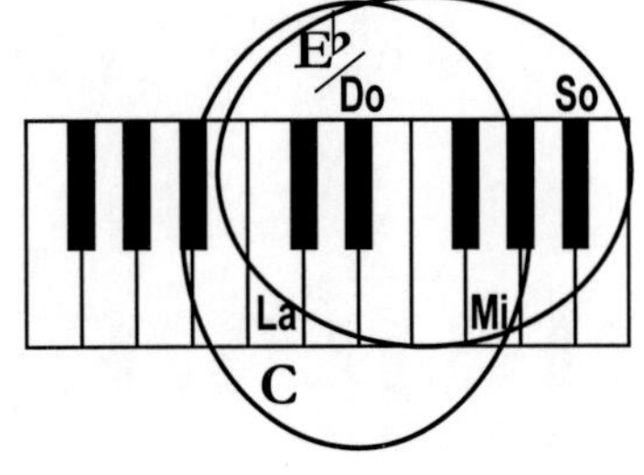

Fingers to Use

Tonic-Dominant-Tonic Arpeggios

Do is E♭

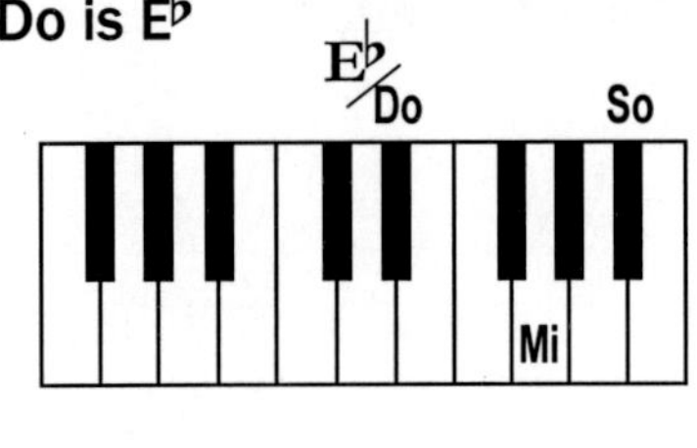

Tonic Major (I)

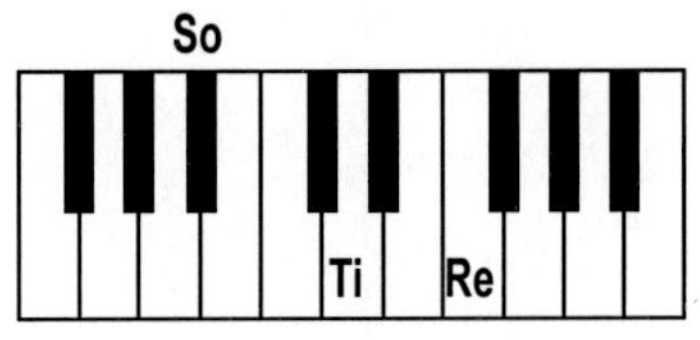

Dominant Major (V)

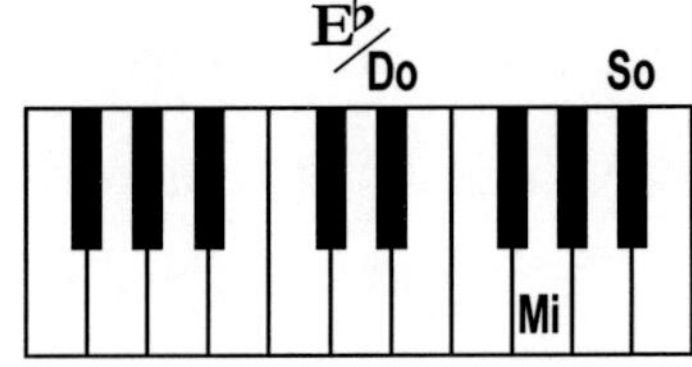

Tonic Major (I)

LA is C

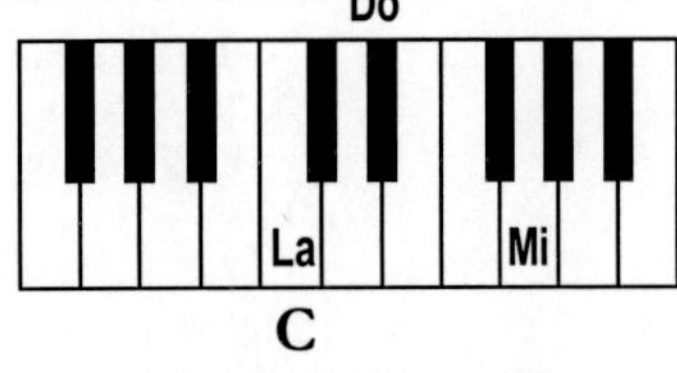

Tonic Minor (i)

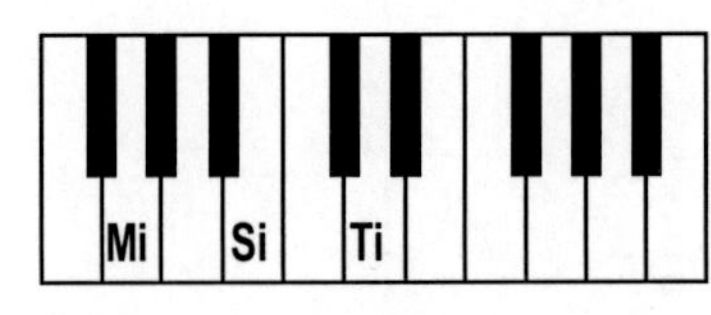

Dominant Harmonic Minor (V)

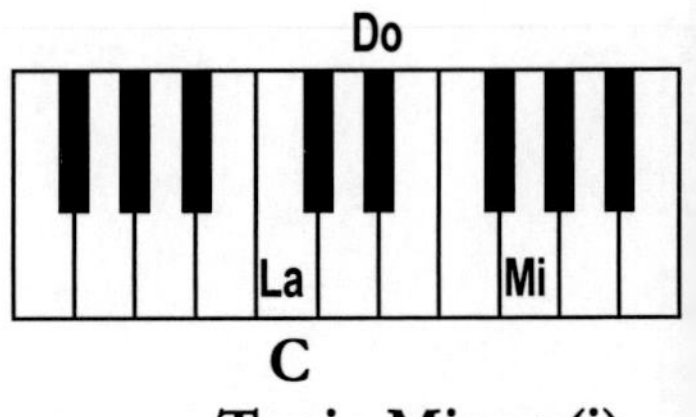

Tonic Minor (i)

Tonic – Subdominant - Tonic
When DO is E♭

Check List

Melodic Cadence

Lesson		Home
________	Hand	________
________	Hand	________
________	Separated	________
________	Connected	________
________	Sing Syllables	________
________	Play I-IV-V-I	________
________	Add LH Roots	________

Arpeggios

Lesson		Home
________	Separated	________
________	Connected	________
________	Sing Syllables	________
________	Play I-IV-V-I	________

Melodic Cadence

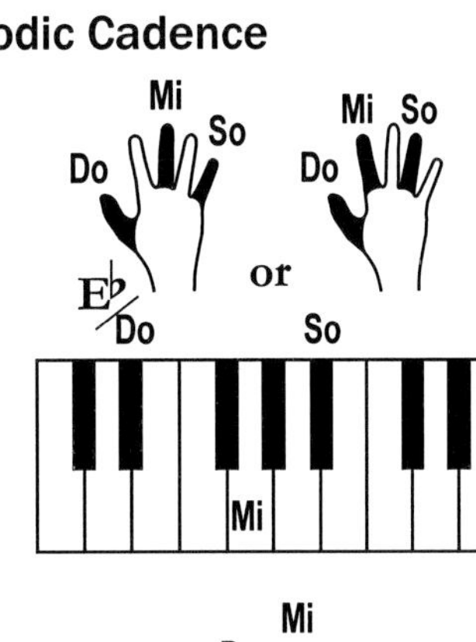

Tonic Major (I)

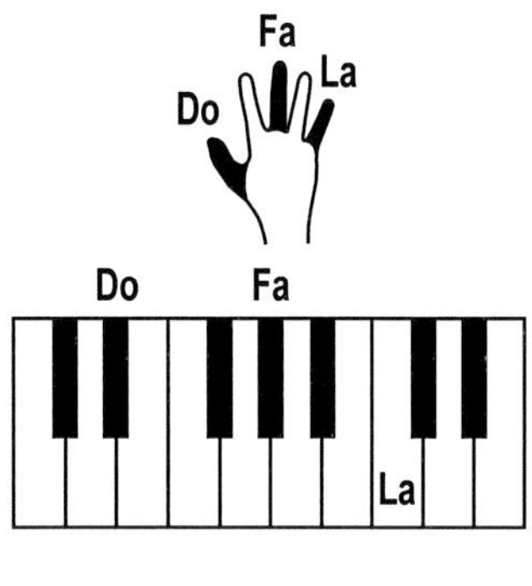

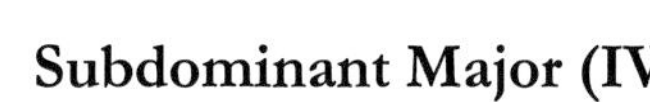

Subdominant Major (IV)

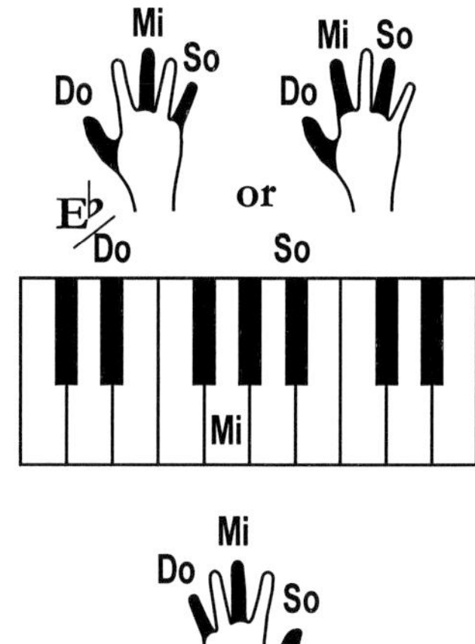

Tonic Major (I)

Arpeggios

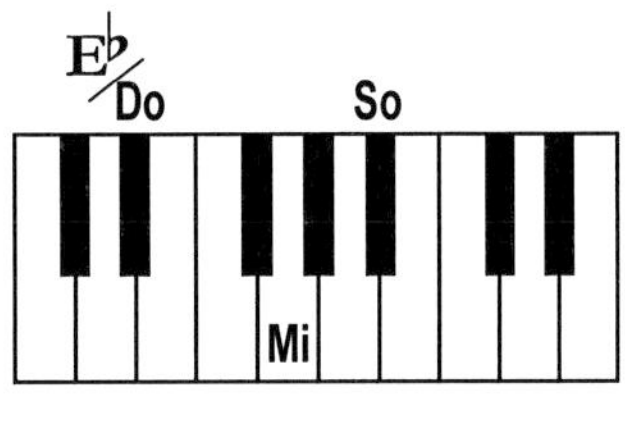

Tonic Major (I)

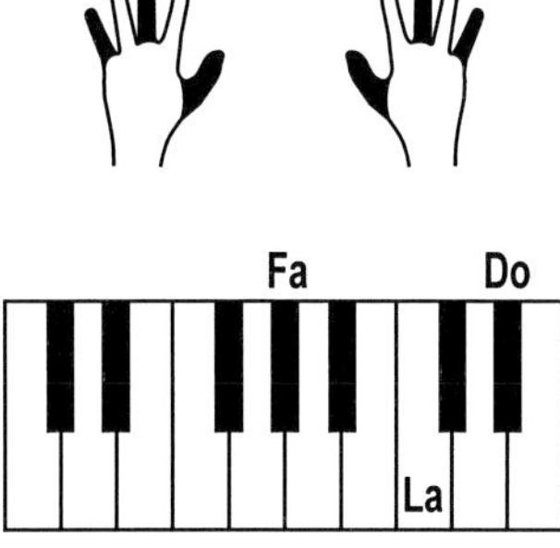

Subdominant Major (IV)

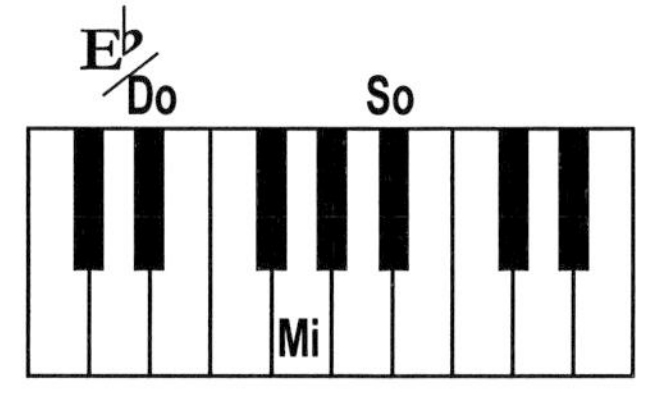

Tonic Major (I)

Tonic – Subdominant - Tonic
When LA is C

Check List

Melodic Cadence

Lesson		Home
________	Hand	________
________	Hand	________
________	Separated	________
________	Connected	________
________	Sing Syllables	________
________	Play i-iv-V-i	________
________	Add LH Roots	________

Arpeggios

Lesson		Home
________	Separated	________
________	Connected	________
________	Sing Syllables	________
________	Play i-iv-V-i	________

Melodic Cadence

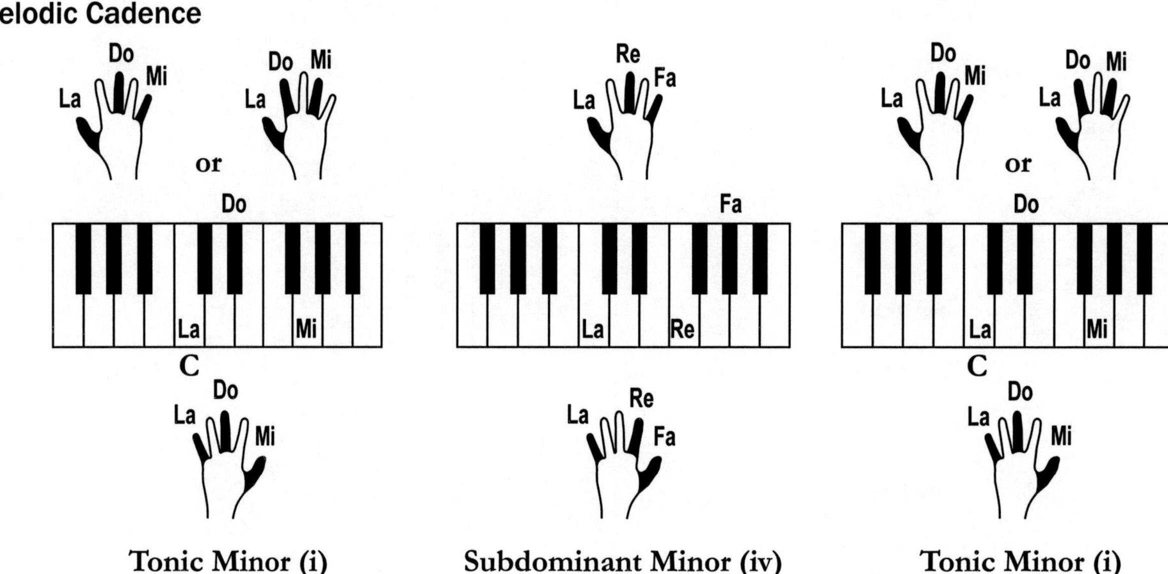

Tonic Minor (i) Subdominant Minor (iv) Tonic Minor (i)

Arpeggios

Fingers to Use

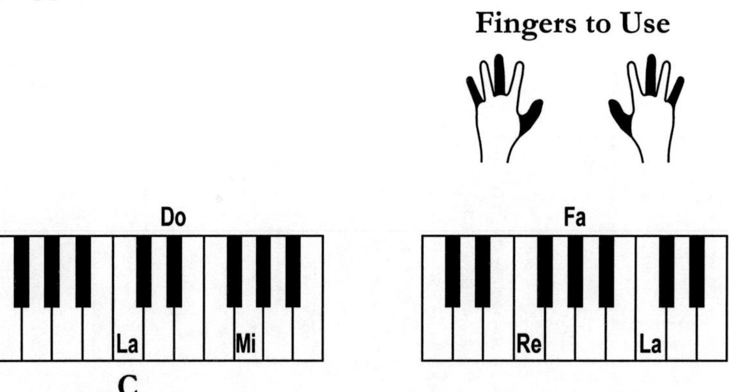

Tonic Minor (i) Subdominant Minor (iv) Tonic Minor (i)

Check List

Tonic Arpeggio

Lesson		Home
______	Separated	______
______	Connected	______
______	Sing Syllables	______

Melodic Cadence

Lesson		Home
______	Hand	______
______	Hand	______
______	Separated	______
______	Connected	______
______	Sing Syllables	______
______	Add LH Roots	______

Transposition

Lesson		Home
______	Folk Song	______
______	Folk Song	______
______	Solo	______
______	Solo	______

Major Tonality – When DO is A♭

Tonic Arpeggio

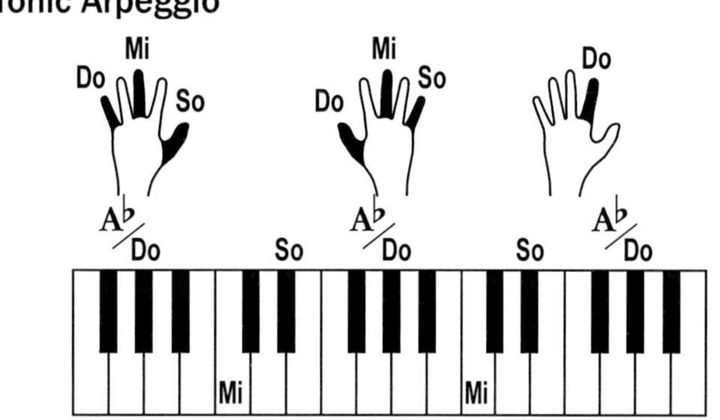

This picture is the keyboard "look" and "feel" of an A♭ Major arpeggio: B W B

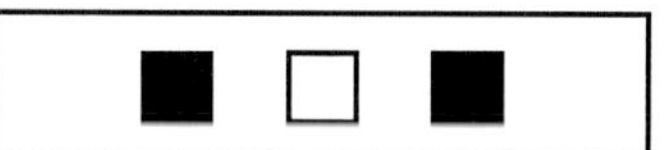

Tonic-Dominant-Tonic Melodic Cadence

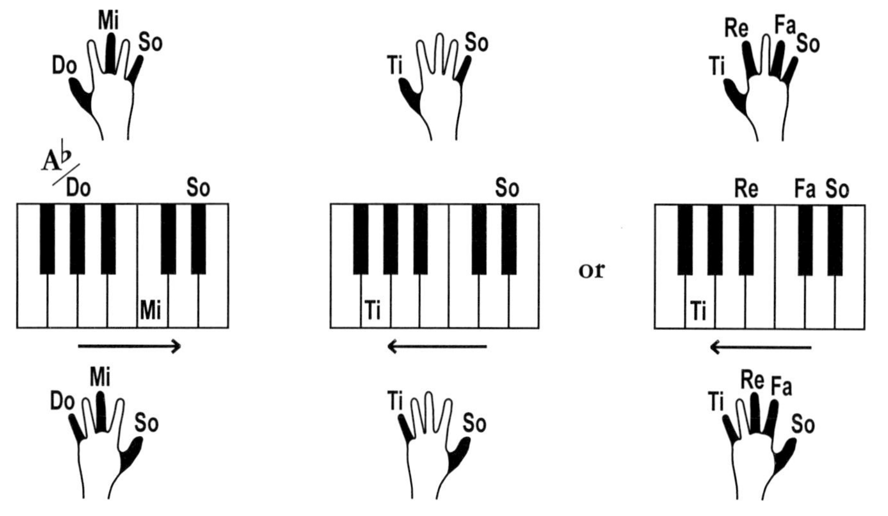

Tonic Major (I) Dominant Major (V) Tonic Major (I)

A♭ Major Scale

DO is A♭

Play the scale with one finger.

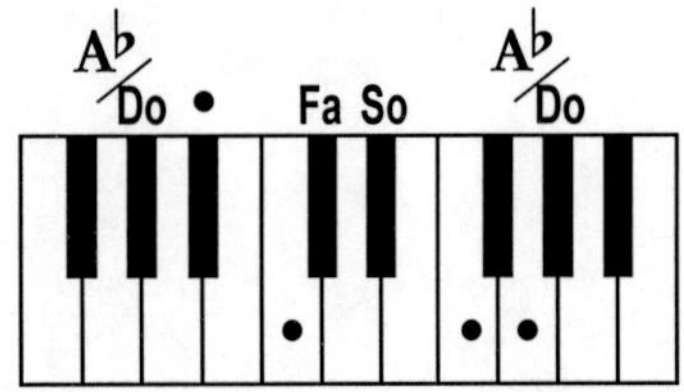

This picture is the keyboard "look" and "feel" of an A♭ Major scale:
B B W B B W W B

Check List

Major Scale

Lesson		Home
________	Hand (right)	________
________	Hand (left)	________
________	Separated	________
________	Connected	________
________	One Octave	________
________	Two Octaves	________
________	Three Octaves	________
________	Four Octaves	________

Learn the thumb crossings.

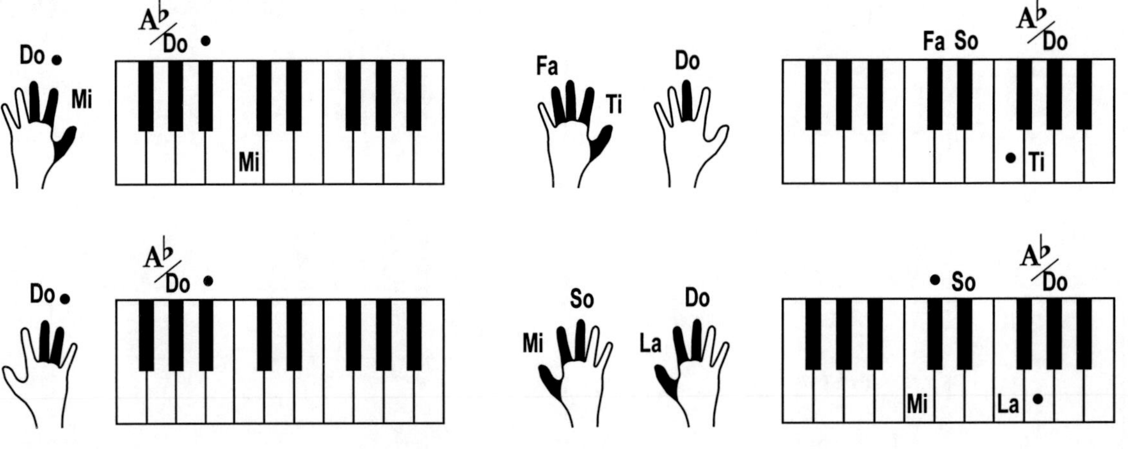

Play the scale from DO to DO.

Harmonic Minor Tonality – When LA is F

Check List

Tonic Arpeggio

Lesson		Home
________	Separated	________
________	Connected	________
________	Sing Syllables	________

Melodic Cadence

Lesson		Home
________	Hand	________
________	Hand	________
________	Separated	________
________	Connected	________
________	Sing Syllables	________
________	Add LH Roots	________

Transposition

Lesson		Home
________	Folk Song	________
________	Folk Song	________
________	Solo	________
________	Solo	________

Tonic Arpeggio

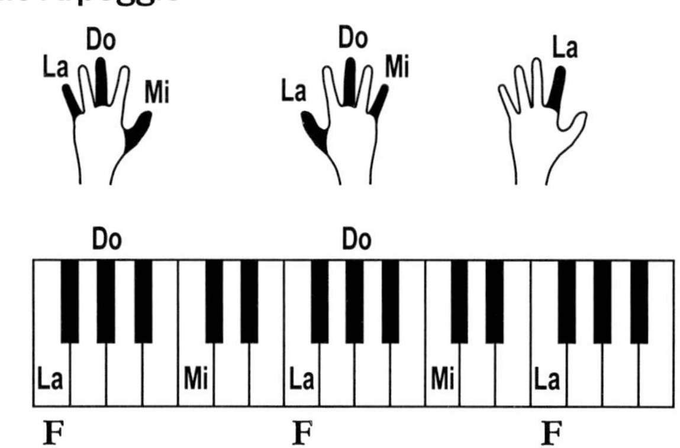

This picture is the keyboard "look" and "feel" of an F Minor arpeggio: W B W

Tonic-Dominant-Tonic Melodic Cadence

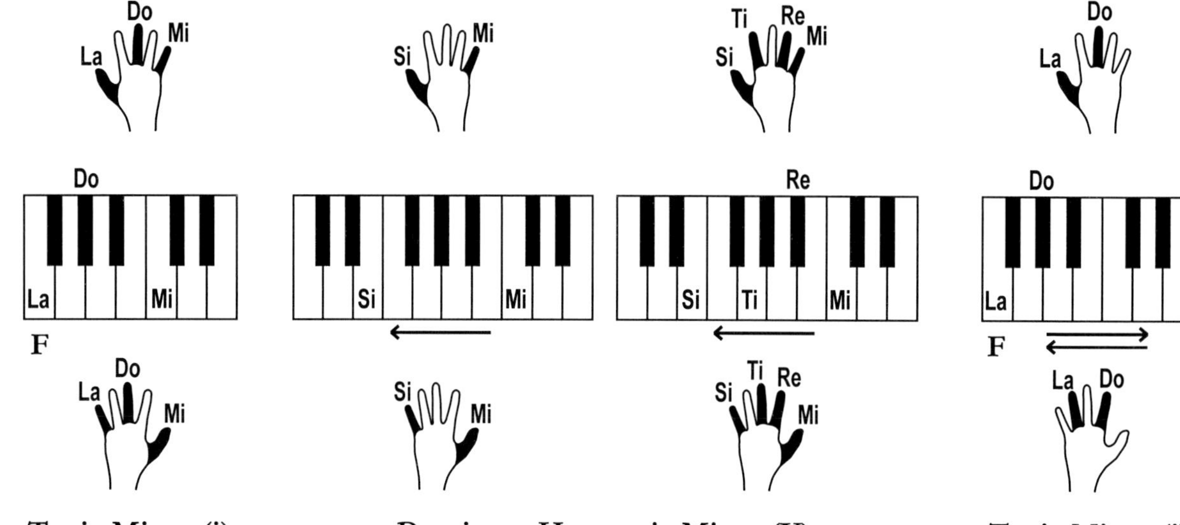

Tonic Minor (i) Dominant Harmonic Minor (V) Tonic Minor (i)

Tonic – Dominant - Tonic Arpeggios
When DO is A♭ then LA is F

Check List

Major Tonality

Lesson		Home
________	Separated	________
________	Connected	________
________	Sing Syllables	________

Harmonic Minor Tonality

Lesson		Home
________	Separated	________
________	Connected	________
________	Sing Syllables	________

When DO is A♭ then LA is F

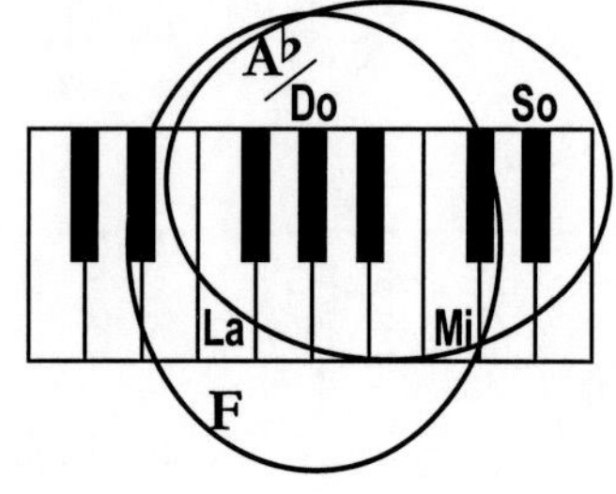

Fingers to Use

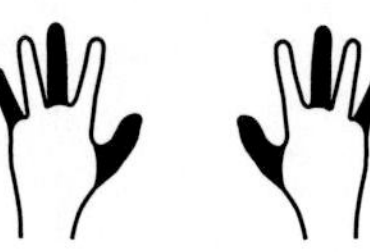

Tonic-Dominant-Tonic Arpeggios

Do is A♭

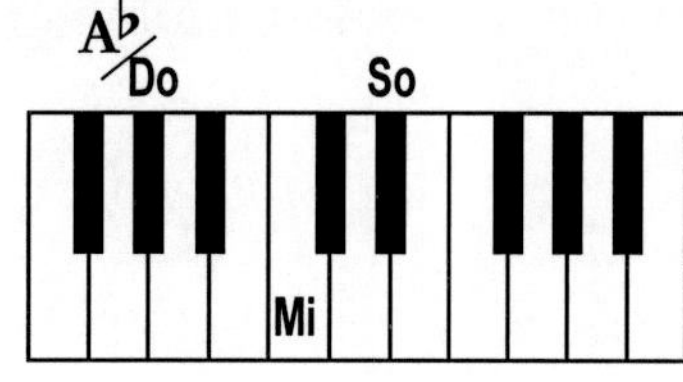

Tonic Major (I)

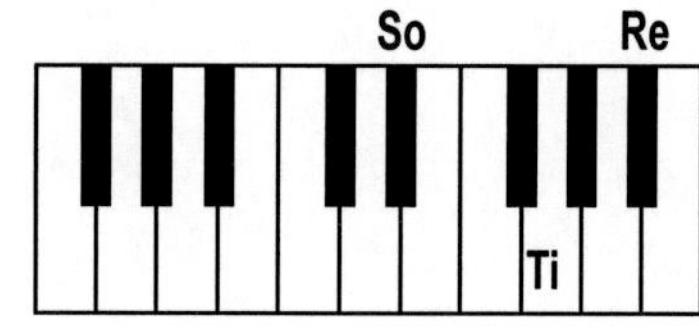

Dominant Major (V)

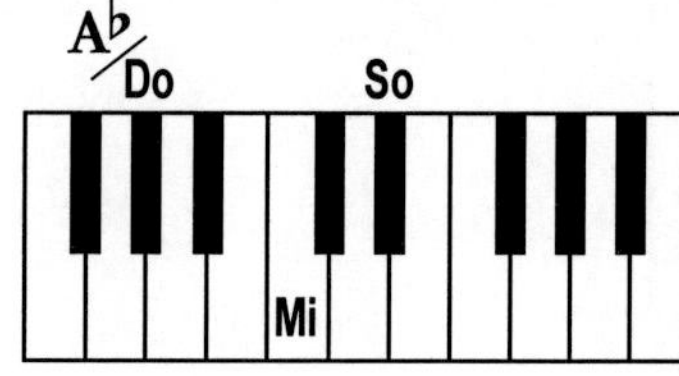

Tonic Major (I)

LA is F

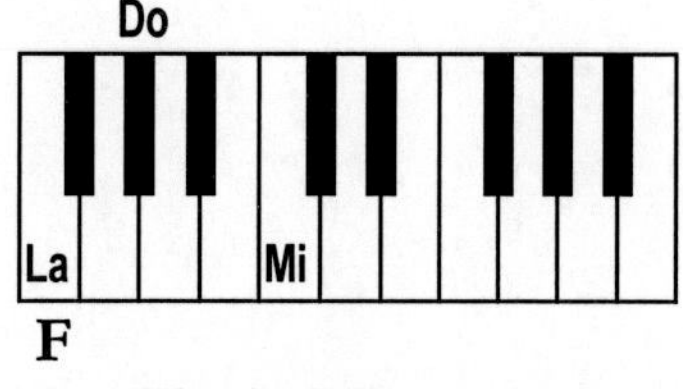

Tonic Minor (i)

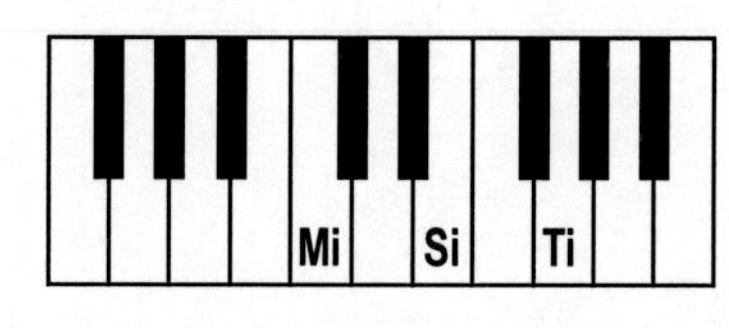

Dominant Harmonic Minor (V)

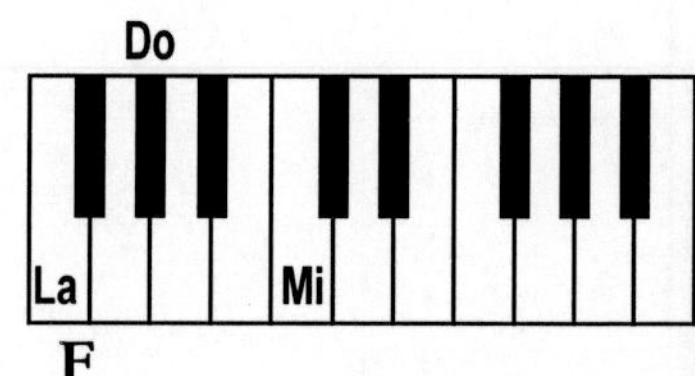

Tonic Minor (i)

Tonic – Subdominant - Tonic
When DO is A♭

Check List

Melodic Cadence

Lesson		Home
________	Hand	________
________	Hand	________
________	Separated	________
________	Connected	________
________	Sing Syllables	________
________	Play I-IV-V-I	________
________	Add LH Roots	________

Arpeggios

Lesson		Home
________	Separated	________
________	Connected	________
________	Sing Syllables	________
________	Play I-IV-V-I	________

Melodic Cadence

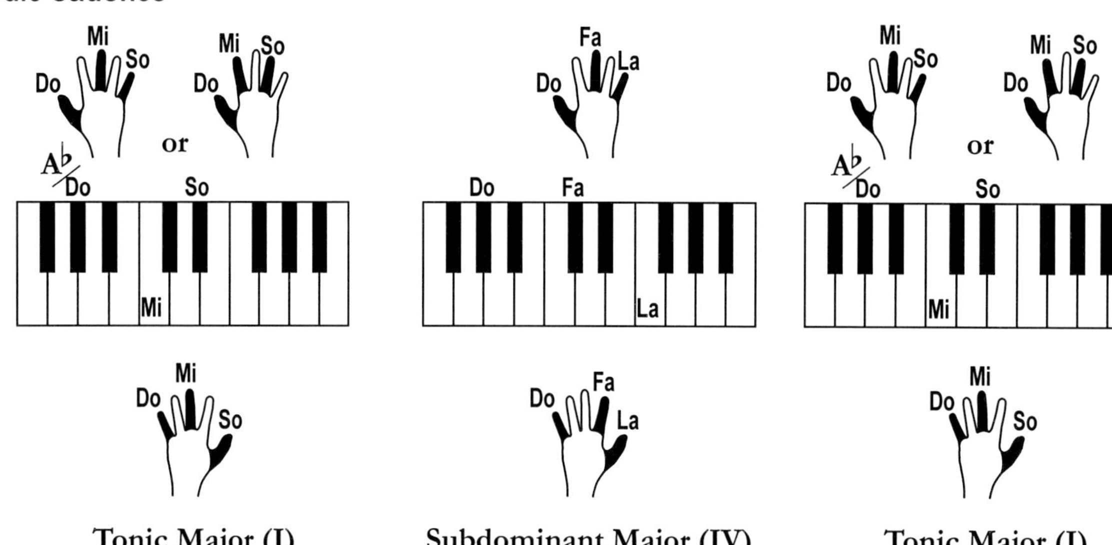

Tonic Major (I) | Subdominant Major (IV) | Tonic Major (I)

Arpeggios

Fingers to Use

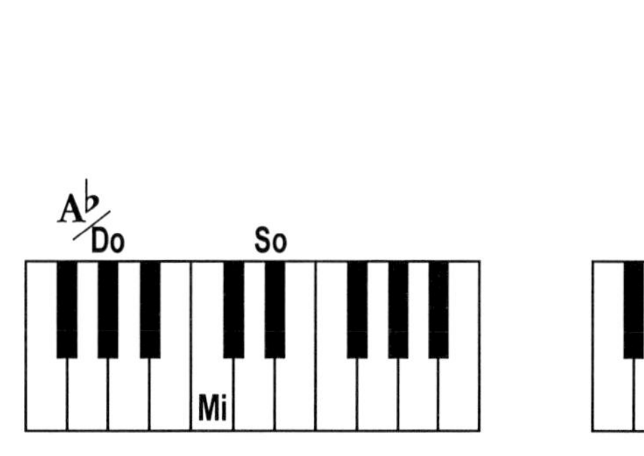

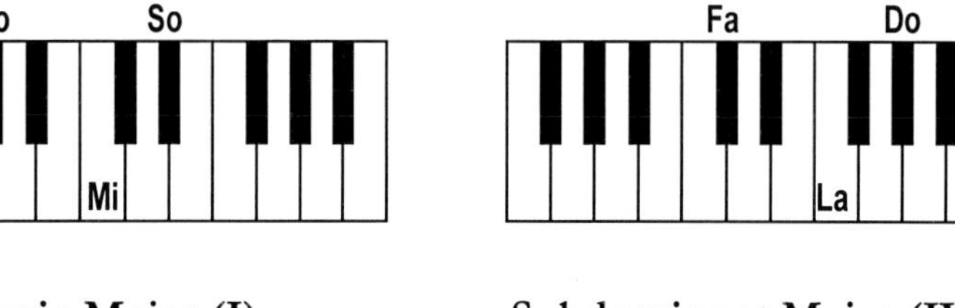

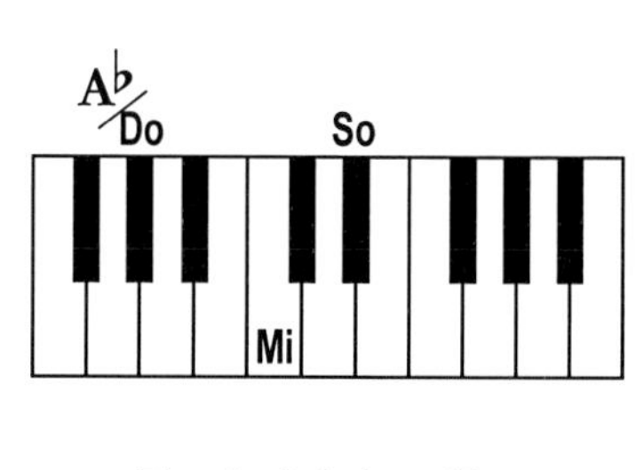

Tonic Major (I) | Subdominant Major (IV) | Tonic Major (I)

Tonic – Subdominant - Tonic
When LA is F

Check List

Melodic Cadence

Lesson		Home
________	Hand	________
________	Hand	________
________	Separated	________
________	Connected	________
________	Sing Syllables	________
________	Play i-iv-V-i	________
________	Add LH Roots	________

Arpeggios

Lesson		Home
________	Separated	________
________	Connected	________
________	Sing Syllables	________
________	Play i-iv-V-i	________

Melodic Cadence

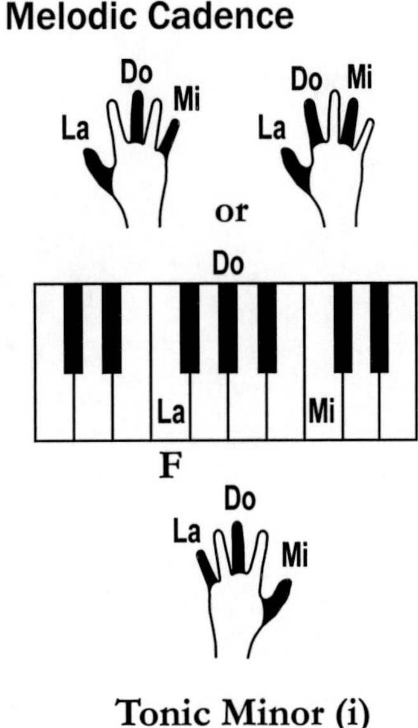

Tonic Minor (i)

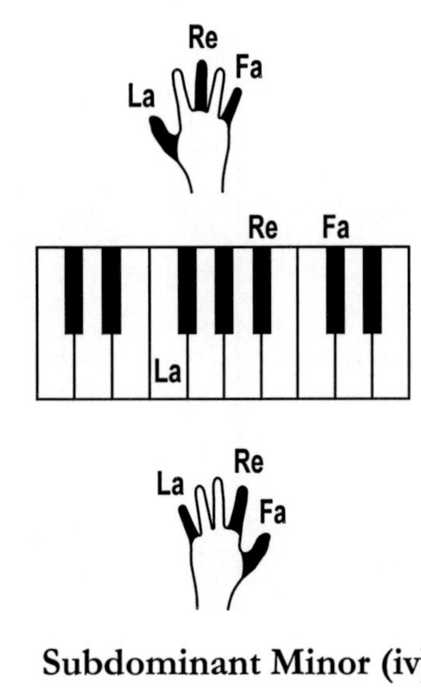

Subdominant Minor (iv)

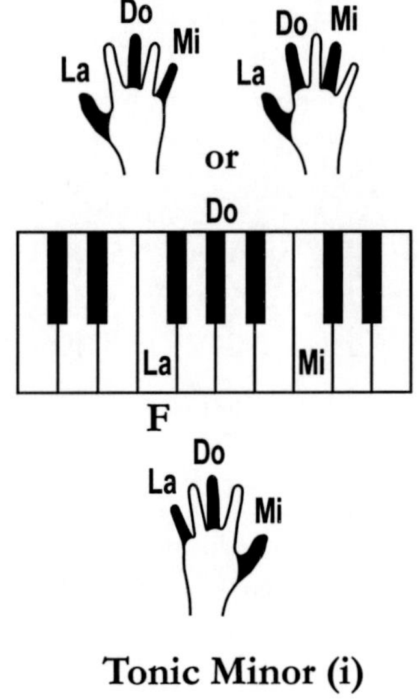

Tonic Minor (i)

Arpeggios

Fingers to Use

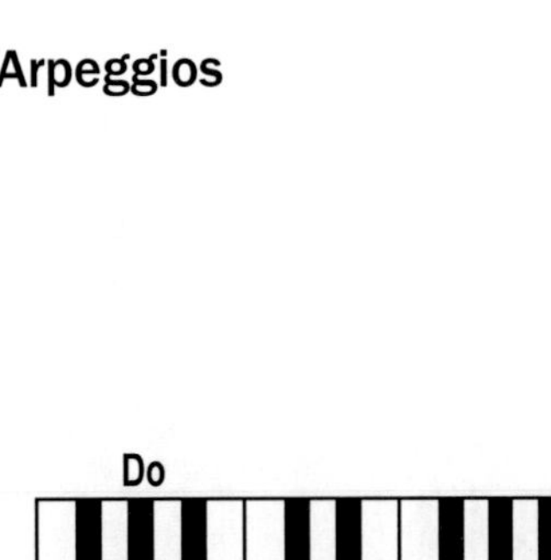

Tonic Minor (i)

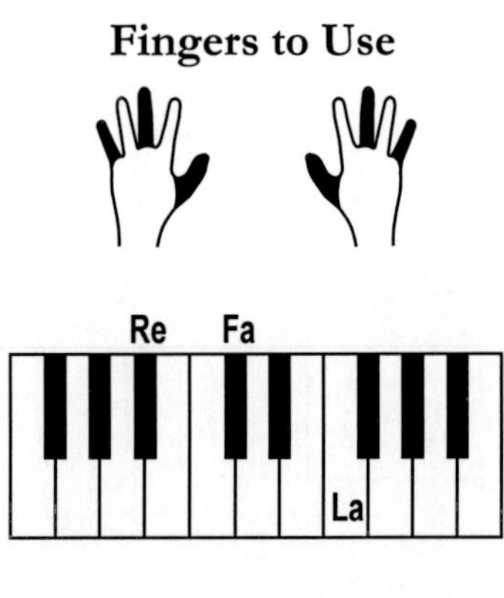

Subdominant Minor (iv)

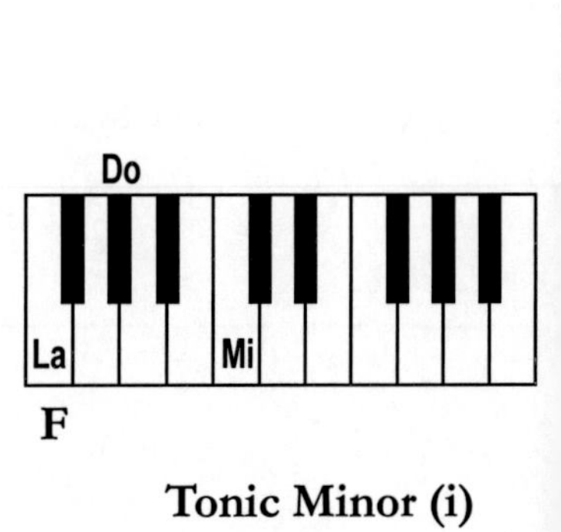

Tonic Minor (i)

Check List

Tonic Arpeggio

Lesson		Home
________	Separated	________
________	Connected	________
________	Sing Syllables	________

Melodic Cadence

Lesson		Home
________	Hand	________
________	Hand	________
________	Separated	________
________	Connected	________
________	Sing Syllables	________
________	Add LH Roots	________

Transposition

Lesson		Home
________	Folk Song	________
________	Folk Song	________
________	Solo	________
________	Solo	________

Major Tonality - When DO is D♭ or C♯

Tonic Arpeggio

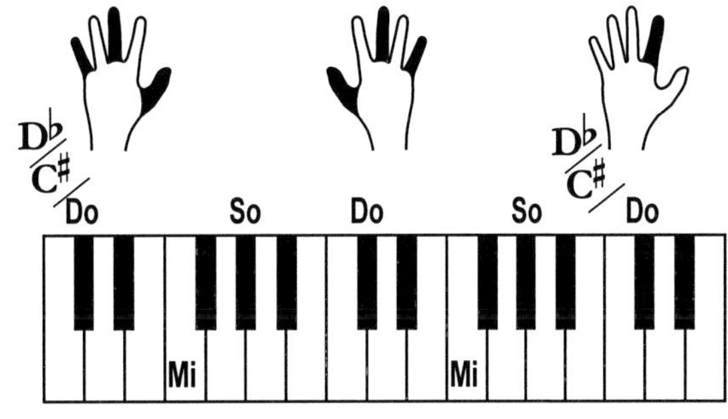

This picture is the keyboard "look" and "feel" of a D♭/C♯ Major arpeggio: B W B

Tonic-Dominant-Tonic Melodic Cadence

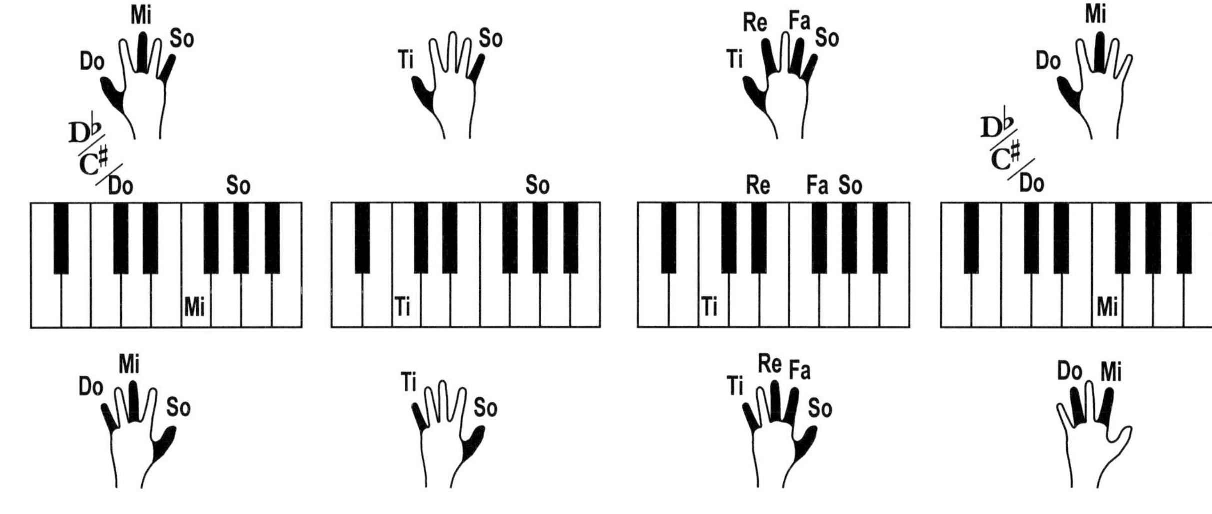

Tonic Major (I) Dominant Major (V) Tonic Major (I)

D♭/C♯ Major Scale

DO is D♭

DO is C♯

Play the scale with one finger.

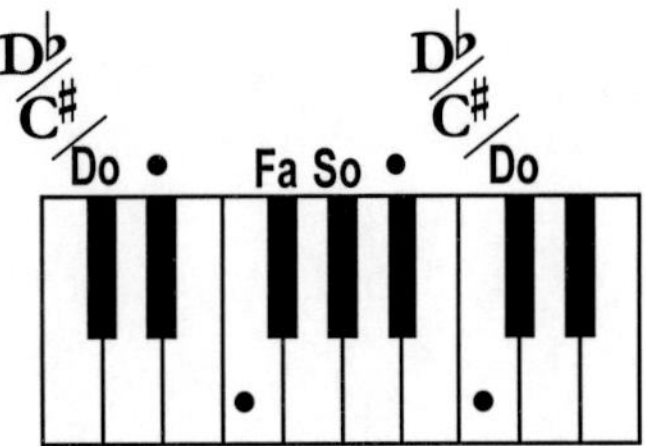

This picture is the keyboard "look" and "feel" of a D♭/C♯ Major scale:
B B W B B B W B

Check List

Major Scale

Lesson		Home
________	Hand (right)	________
________	Hand (left)	________
________	Separated	________
________	Connected	________
________	One Octave	________
________	Two Octaves	________
________	Three Octaves	________
________	Four Octaves	________

Learn the thumb crossings.

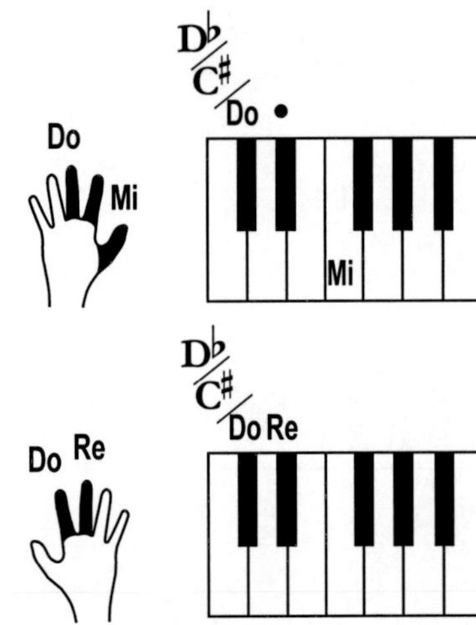

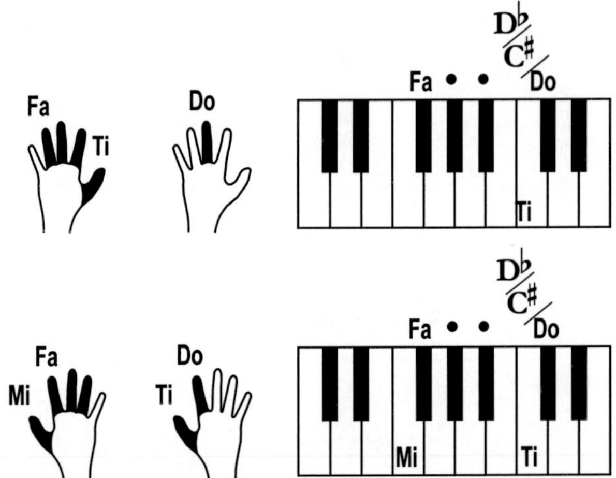

Play the scale from DO to DO.

Harmonic Minor Tonality – When LA is B♭

Check List		
Tonic Arpeggio		
Lesson		Home
________	Separated	________
________	Connected	________
________	Sing Syllables	________
Melodic Cadence		
Lesson		Home
________	Hand	________
________	Hand	________
________	Separated	________
________	Connected	________
________	Sing Syllables	________
________	Add LH Roots	________
Transposition		
Lesson		Home
________	Folk Song	________
________	Folk Song	________
________	Solo	________
________	Solo	________

Tonic Arpeggio

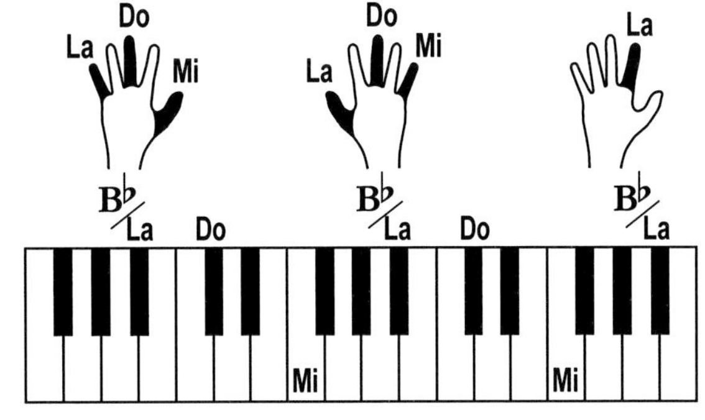

This picture is the keyboard "look" and "feel" of a B♭ Minor arpeggio: B B W

Tonic-Dominant-Tonic Melodic Cadence

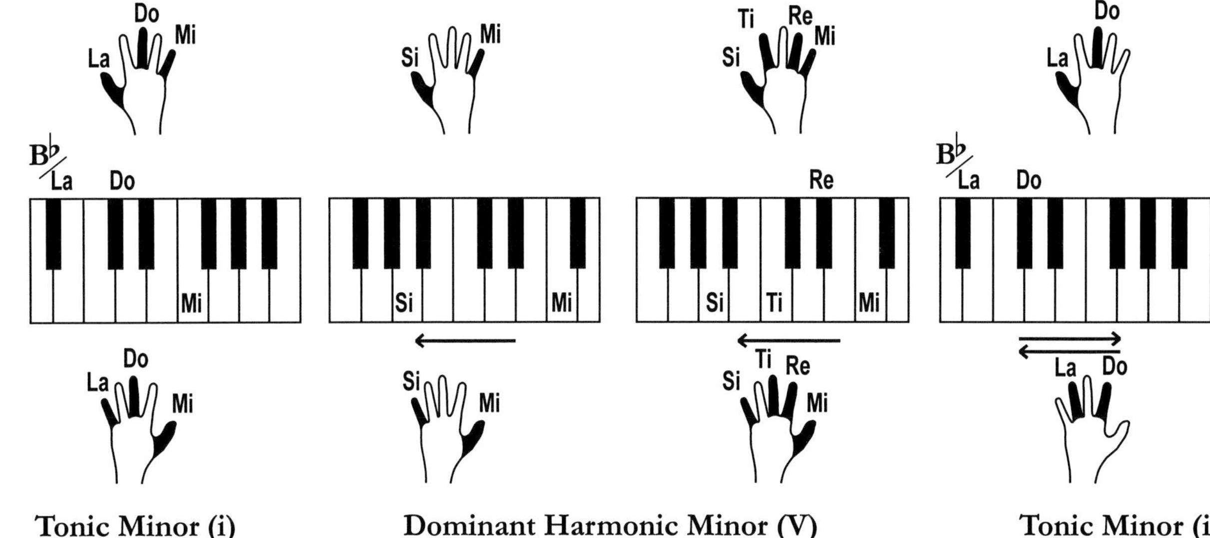

Tonic Minor (i) Dominant Harmonic Minor (V) Tonic Minor (i)

Tonic – Dominant - Tonic Arpeggios
When DO is D♭/C♯ then LA is B♭

Check List		
Major Tonality		
Lesson		Home
________	Separated	________
________	Connected	________
________	Sing Syllables	________
Harmonic Minor Tonality		
Lesson		Home
________	Separated	________
________	Connected	________
________	Sing Syllables	________

When DO is D♭/C♯ then LA is B♭

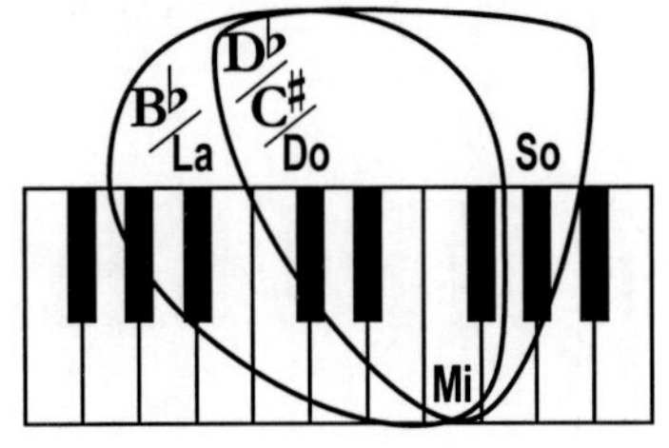

Fingers to Use

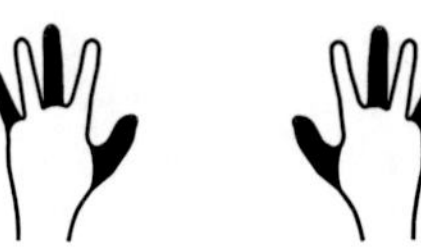

Tonic-Dominant-Tonic Arpeggios

Do is D♭/C♯

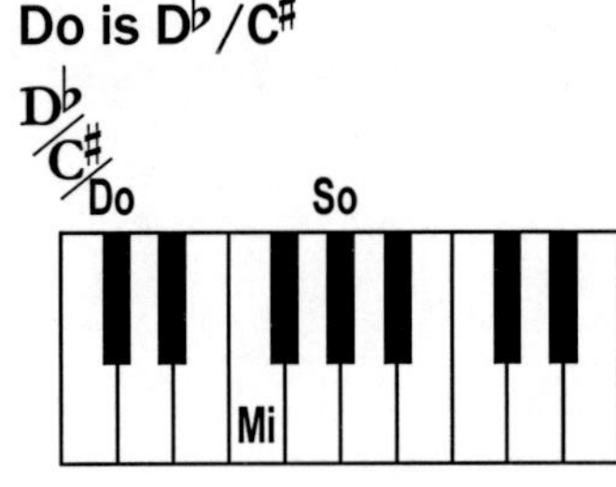

Tonic Major (I)

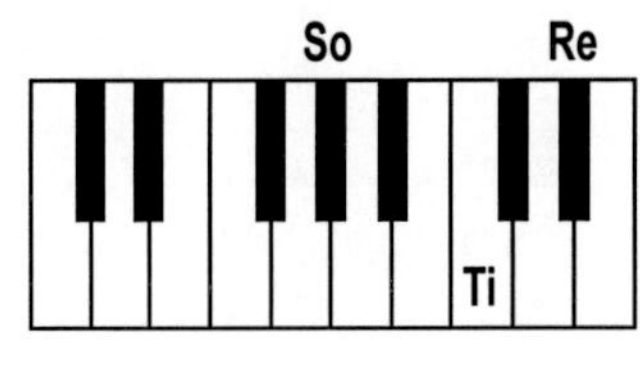

Dominant Major (V)

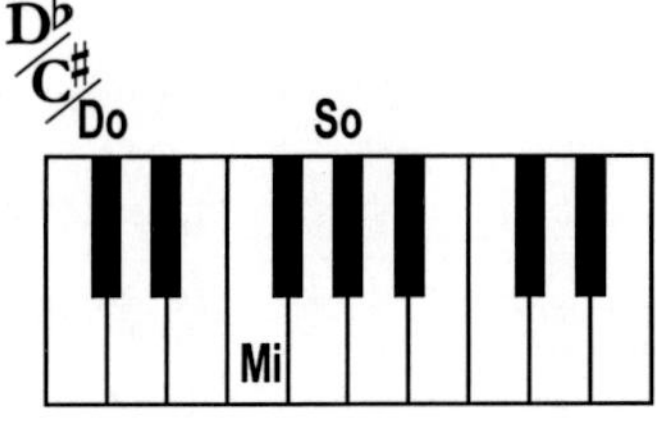

Tonic Major (I)

LA is B♭

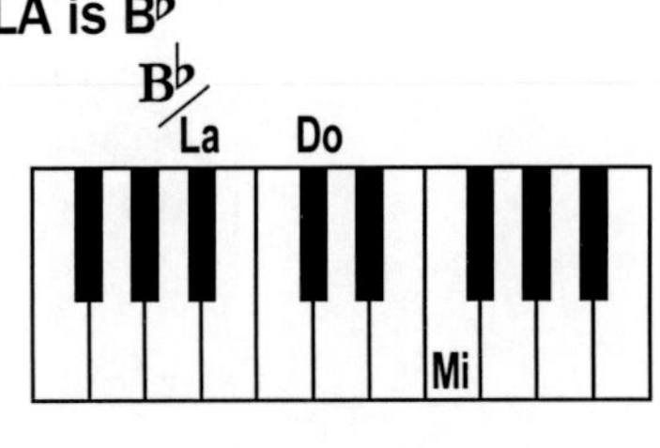

Tonic Minor (i)

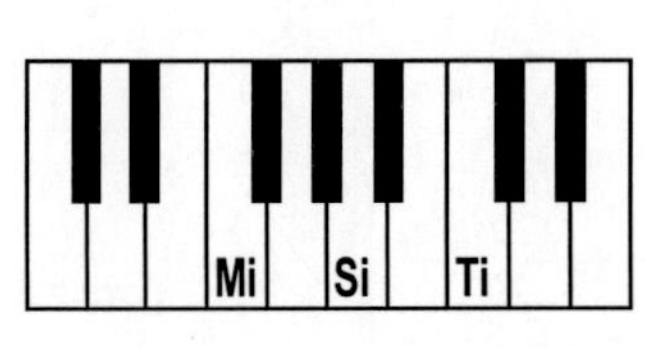

Dominant Harmonic Minor (V)

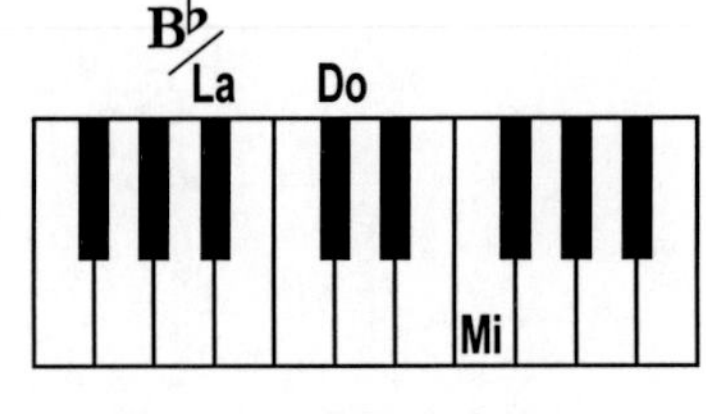

Tonic Minor (i)

Tonic – Subdominant - Tonic
When DO is D♭/C♯

Check List

Melodic Cadence

Lesson		Home
________	Hand	________
________	Hand	________
________	Separated	________
________	Connected	________
________	Sing Syllables	________
________	Play I-IV-V-I	________
________	Add LH Roots	________

Arpeggios

Lesson		Home
________	Separated	________
________	Connected	________
________	Sing Syllables	________
________	Play I-IV-V-I	________

Melodic Cadence

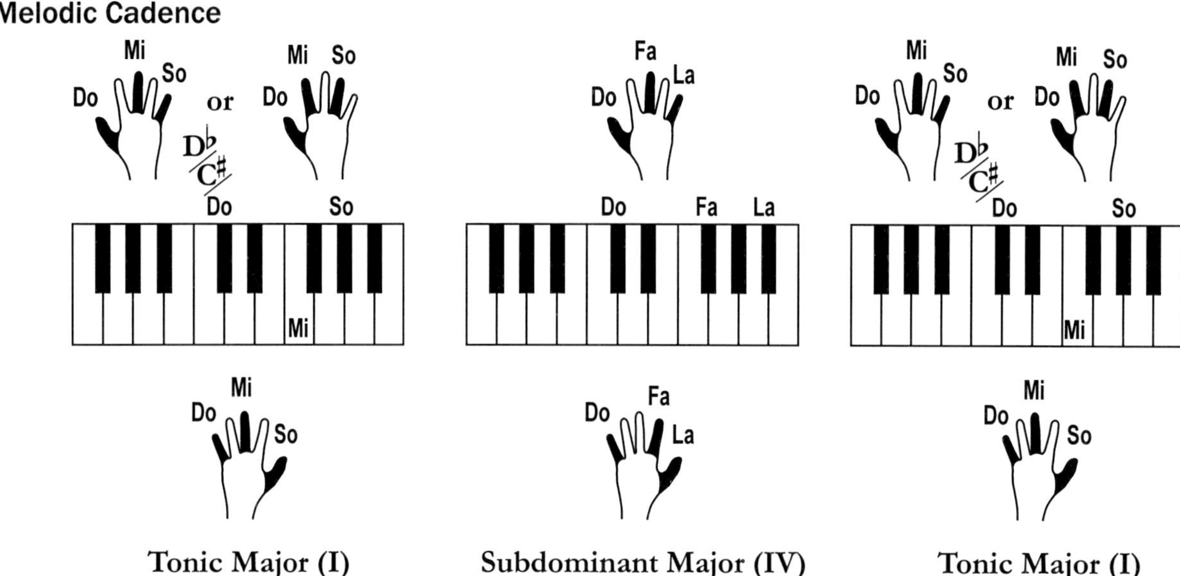

Tonic Major (I) — Subdominant Major (IV) — Tonic Major (I)

Arpeggios

Fingers to Use

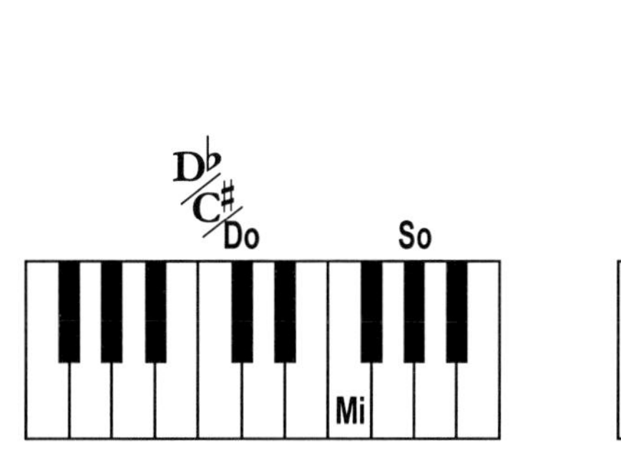

Tonic Major (I)

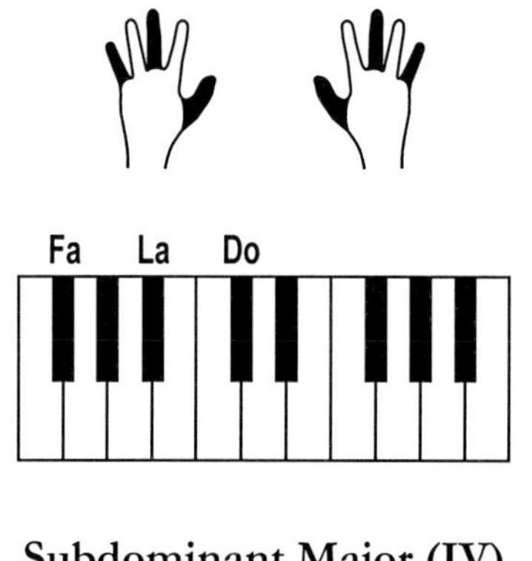

Subdominant Major (IV)

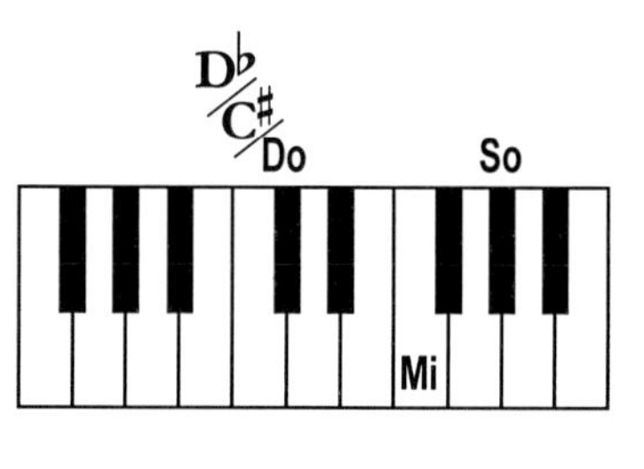

Tonic Major (I)

Tonic – Subdominant - Tonic
When LA is B♭

Check List

Melodic Cadence

Lesson		Home
________	Hand	________
________	Hand	________
________	Separated	________
________	Connected	________
________	Sing Syllables	________
________	Play i-iv-V-i	________
________	Add LH Roots	________

Arpeggios

Lesson		Home
________	Separated	________
________	Connected	________
________	Sing Syllables	________
________	Play i-iv-V-i	________

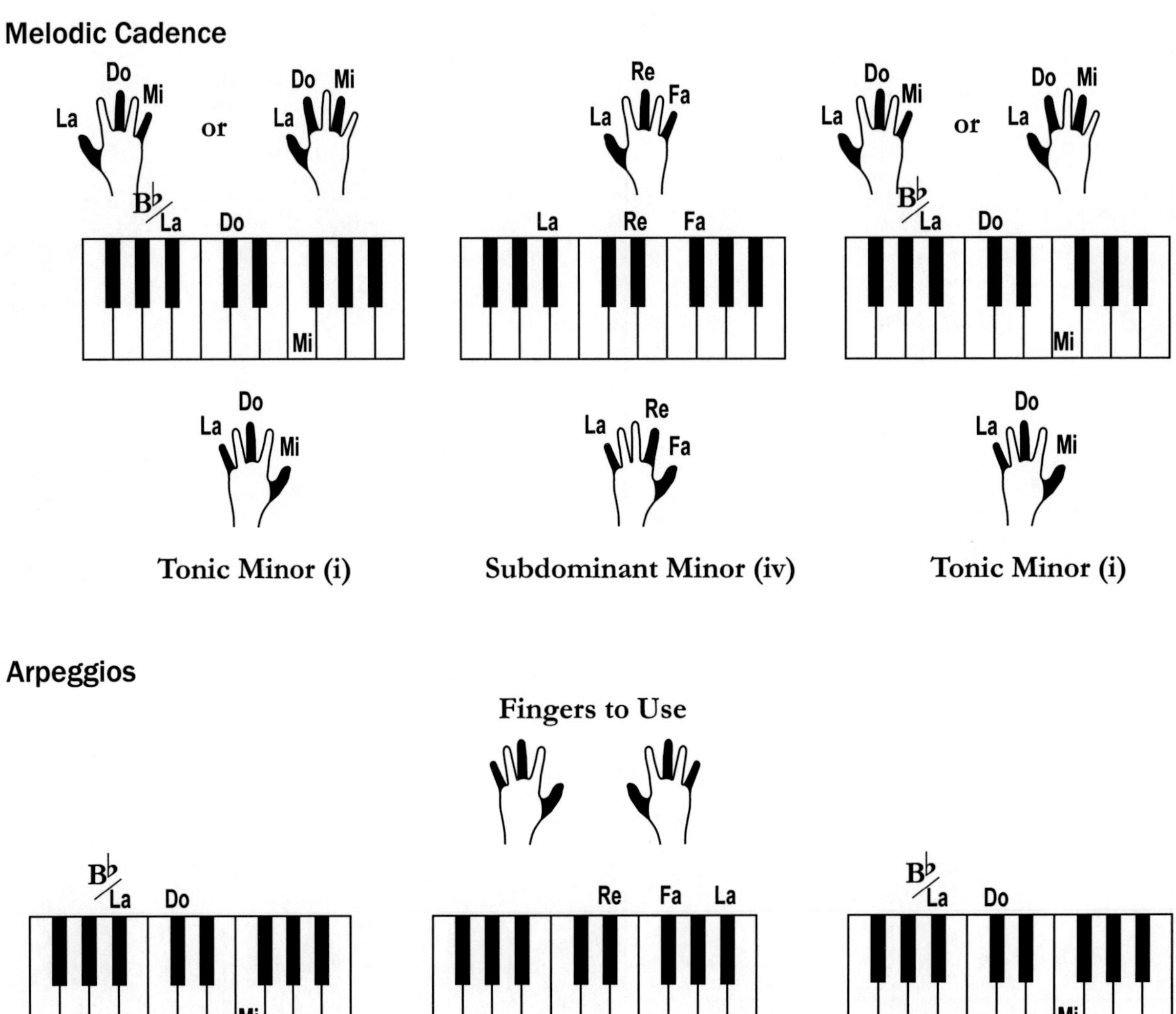

Check List

Tonic Arpeggio

Lesson		Home
________	Separated	________
________	Connected	________
________	Sing Syllables	________

Melodic Cadence

Lesson		Home
________	Hand	________
________	Hand	________
________	Separated	________
________	Connected	________
________	Sing Syllables	________
________	Add LH Roots	________

Transposition

Lesson		Home
________	Folk Song	________
________	Folk Song	________
________	Solo	________
________	Solo	________

Major Tonality – When DO is G♭or F♯

Tonic Arpeggio

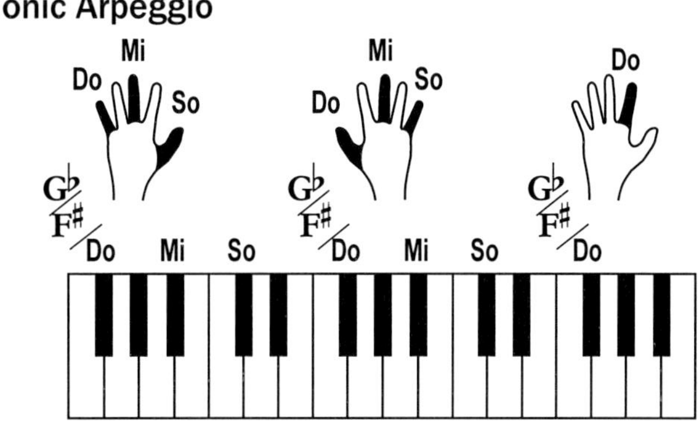

This picture is the keyboard "look" and "feel" of a G♭/F♯ Major arpeggio: B B B

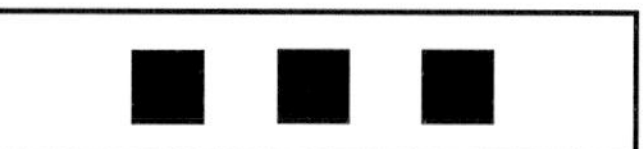

Tonic-Dominant-Tonic Melodic Cadence

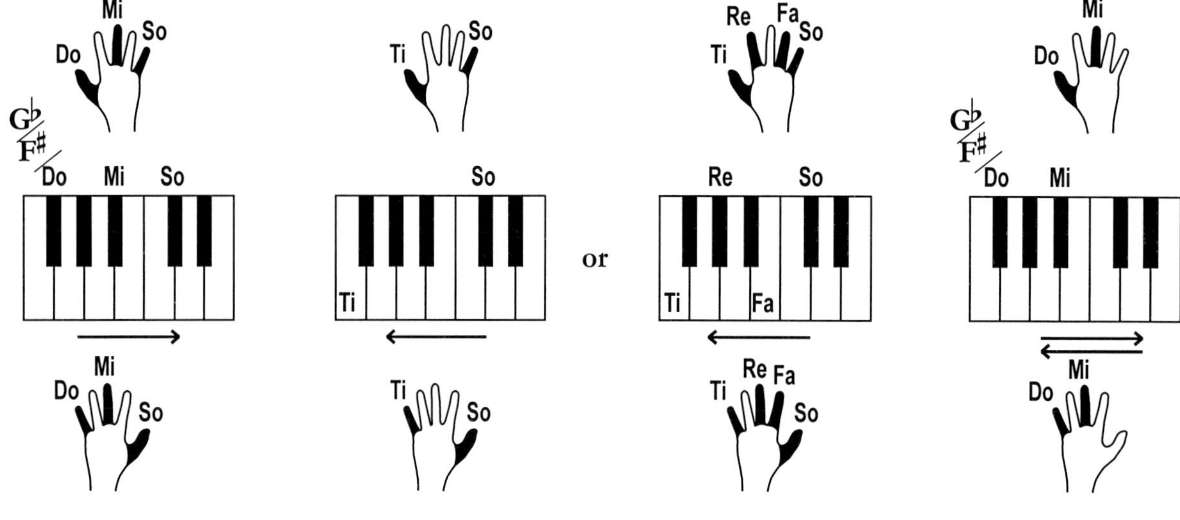

Tonic Major (I) Dominant Major (V) Tonic Major (I)

G♭/F♯ Major Scale

DO is G♭

DO is F♯

Play the scale with one finger.

This picture is the keyboard "look" and "feel" of a G♭/F♯ Major scale:
B B B W B B W B

Check List

Major Scale

Lesson		Home
________	Hand (left)	________
________	Hand (right)	________
________	Separated	________
________	Connected	________
________	One Octave	________
________	Two Octaves	________
________	Three Octaves	________
________	Four Octaves	________

Learn the thumb crossings.

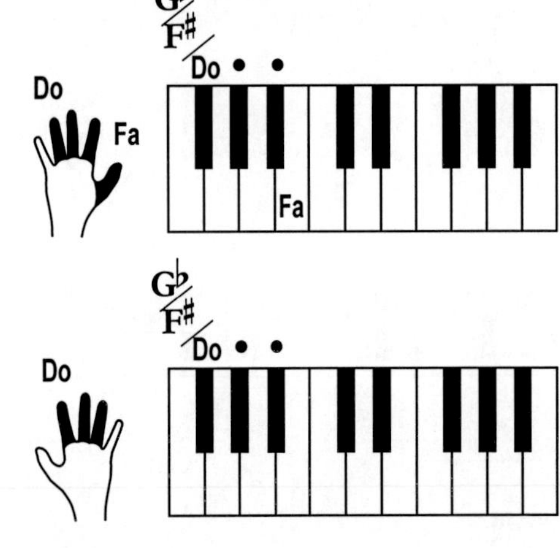

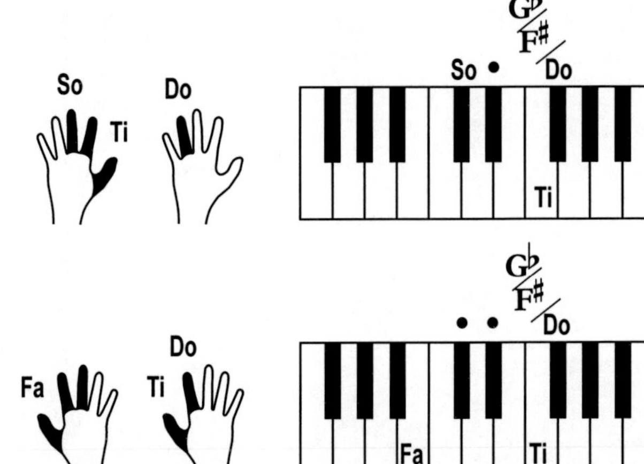

Play the scale from DO to DO.

Harmonic Minor Tonality – When LA is E♭

Check List

Tonic Arpeggio

Lesson		Home
______	Separated	______
______	Connected	______
______	Sing Syllables	______

Melodic Cadence

Lesson		Home
______	Hand	______
______	Hand	______
______	Separated	______
______	Connected	______
______	Sing Syllables	______
______	Add LH Roots	______

Transposition

Lesson		Home
______	Folk Song	______
______	Folk Song	______
______	Solo	______
______	Solo	______

Tonic Arpeggio

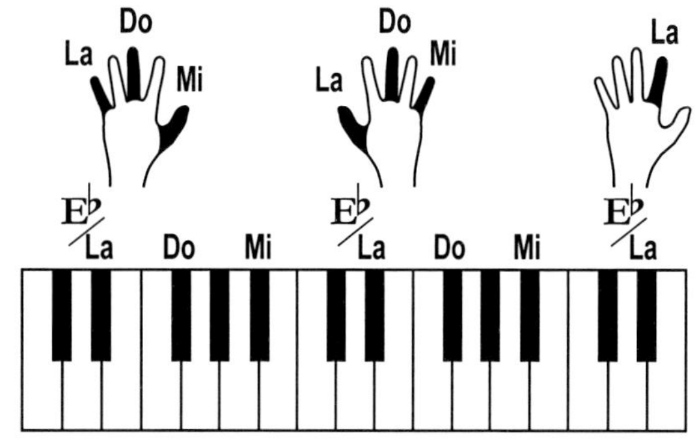

This picture is the keyboard "look" and "feel" of an E♭ Minor arpeggio: B B B

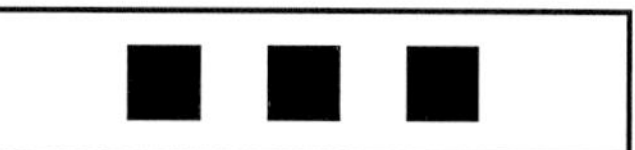

Tonic-Dominant-Tonic Melodic Cadence

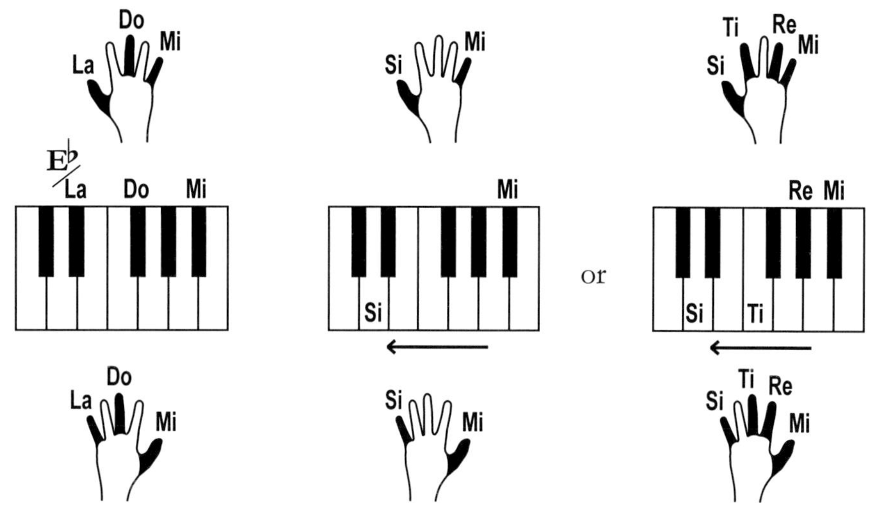

Tonic Minor (i) Dominant Harmonic Minor (V) Tonic Minor (i)

Tonic – Dominant - Tonic Arpeggios
When DO is G♭/F♯ then LA is E♭

Check List

Major Tonality

Lesson		Home
________	Separated	________
________	Connected	________
________	Sing Syllables	________

Harmonic Minor Tonality

Lesson		Home
________	Separated	________
________	Connected	________
________	Sing Syllables	________

When DO is G♭/F♯ then LA is A♭

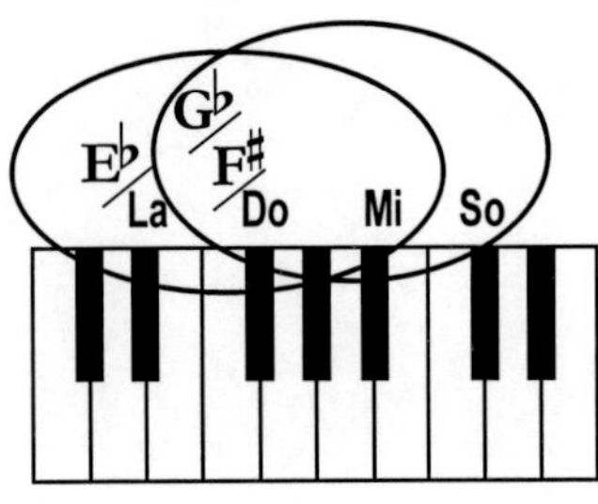

Fingers to Use

Tonic-Dominant-Tonic Arpeggios

Do is G♭/F♯

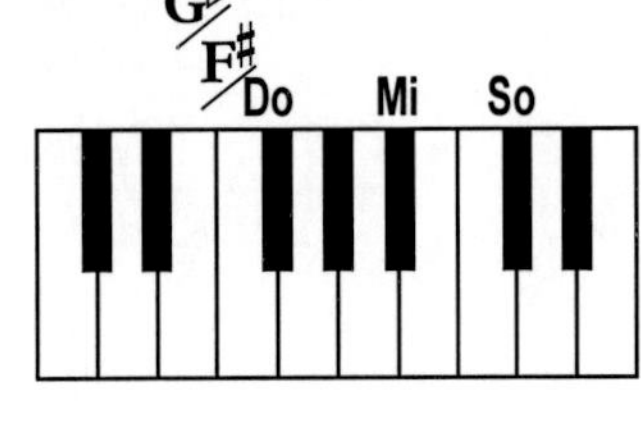

Tonic Major (I)

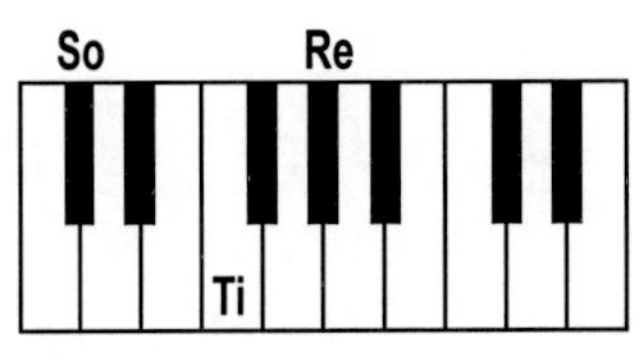

Dominant Major (V)

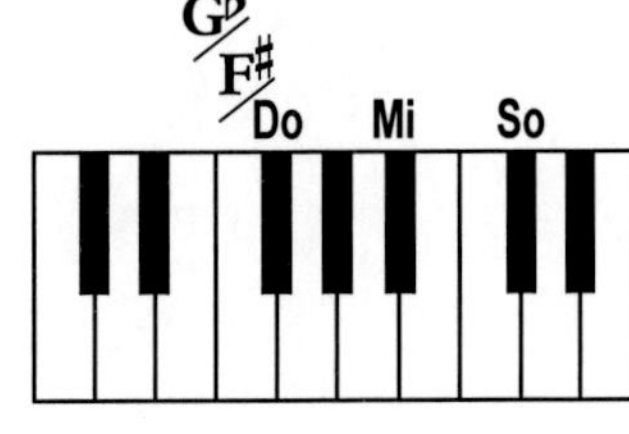

Tonic Major (I)

LA is E♭

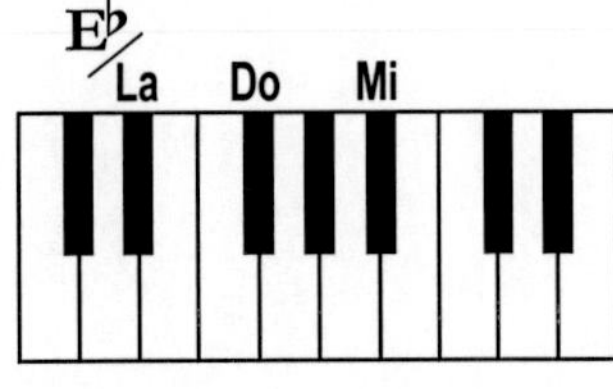

Tonic Minor (i)

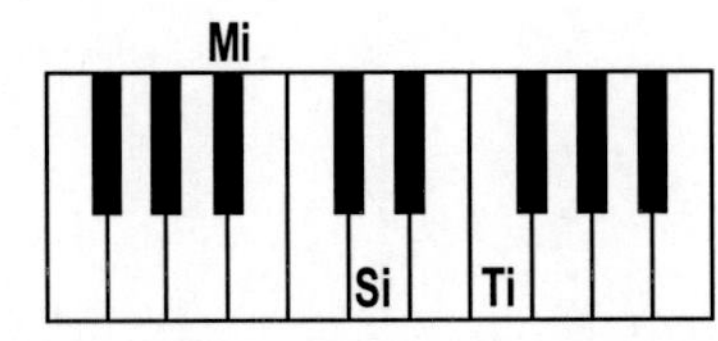

Dominant Harmonic Minor (V)

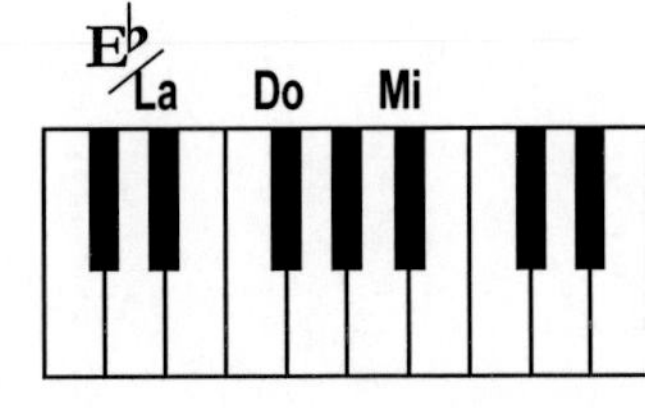

Tonic Minor (i)

Tonic – Subdominant - Tonic
When DO is G♭/F♯

Check List

Melodic Cadence

Lesson		Home
________	Hand	________
________	Hand	________
________	Separated	________
________	Connected	________
________	Sing Syllables	________
________	Play I-IV-V-I	________
________	Add LH Roots	________

Arpeggios

Lesson		Home
________	Separated	________
________	Connected	________
________	Sing Syllables	________
________	Play I-IV-V-I	________

Melodic Cadence

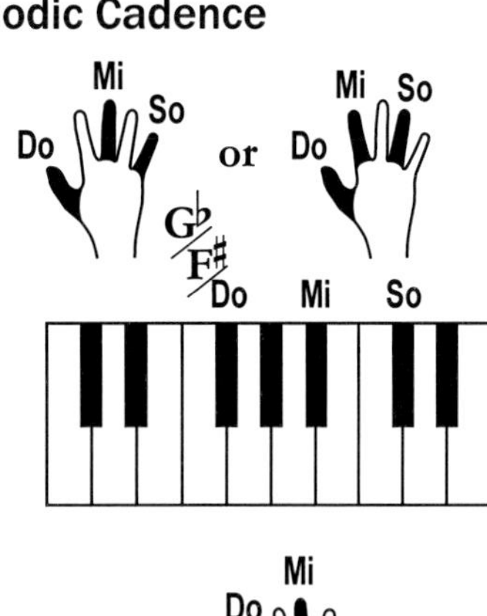

Tonic Major (I)

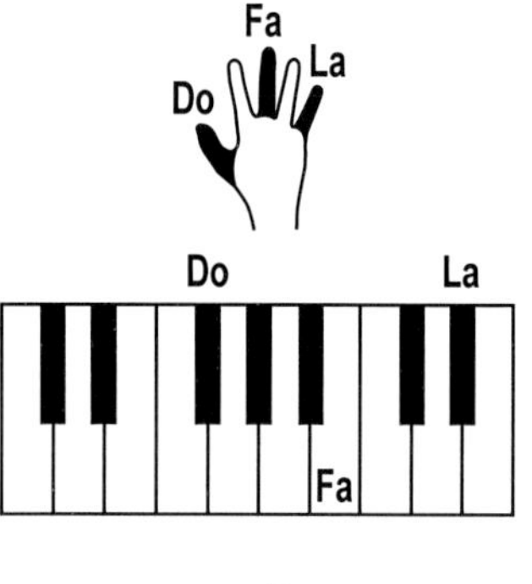

Subdominant Major (IV)

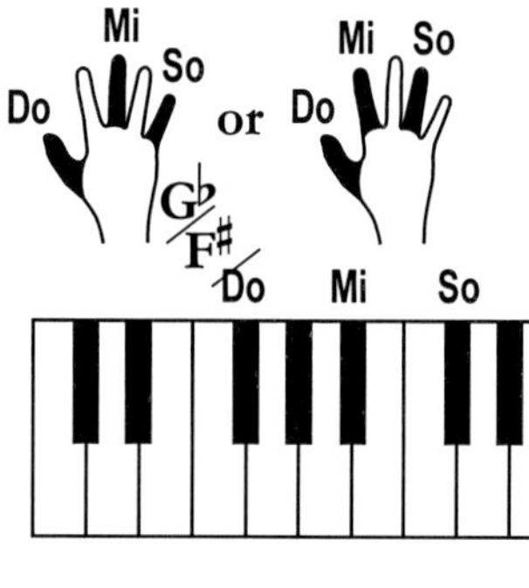

Tonic Major (I)

Arpeggios

Fingers to Use

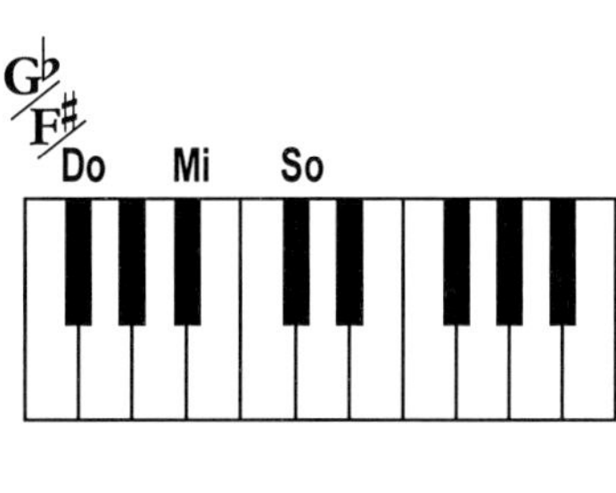

Tonic Major (I)

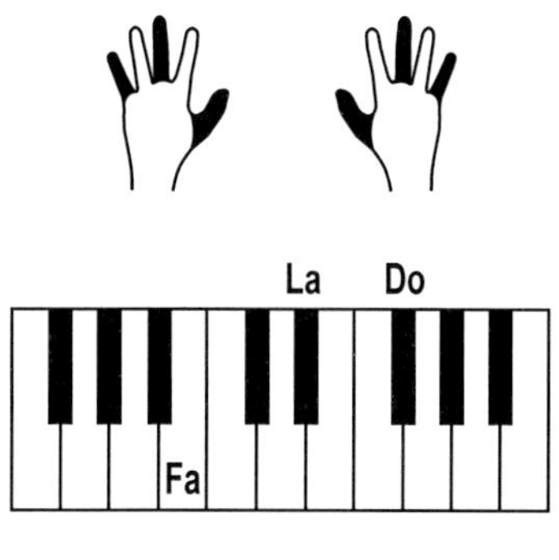

Subdominant Major (IV)

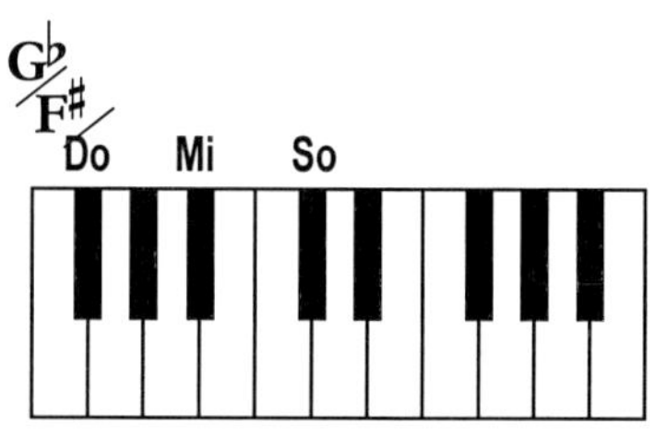

Tonic Major (I)

Tonic – Subdominant - Tonic
When LA is E♭

Check List

Melodic Cadence

Lesson		Home
______	Hand	______
______	Hand	______
______	Separated	______
______	Connected	______
______	Sing Syllables	______
______	Play i-iv-V-i	______
______	Add LH Roots	______

Arpeggios

Lesson		Home
______	Separated	______
______	Connected	______
______	Sing Syllables	______
______	Play i-iv-V-i	______

Melodic Cadence

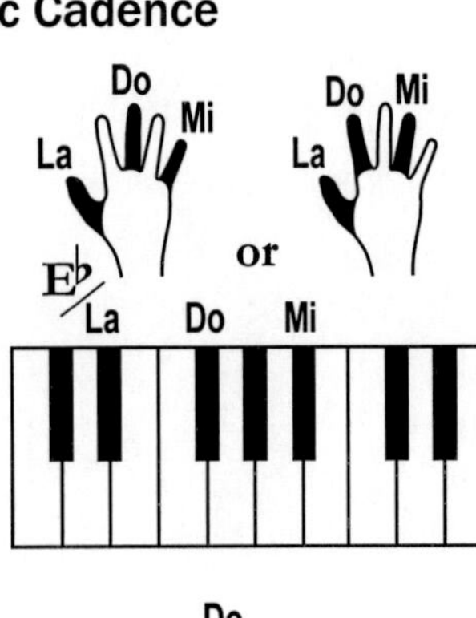

Tonic Minor (i)

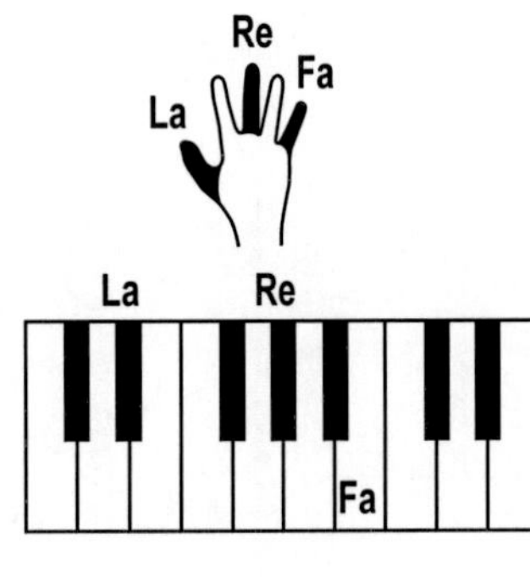

Subdominant Minor (iv)

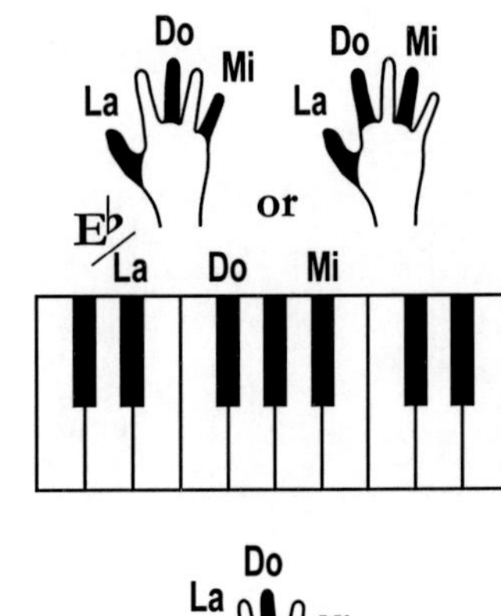

Tonic Minor (i)

Arpeggios

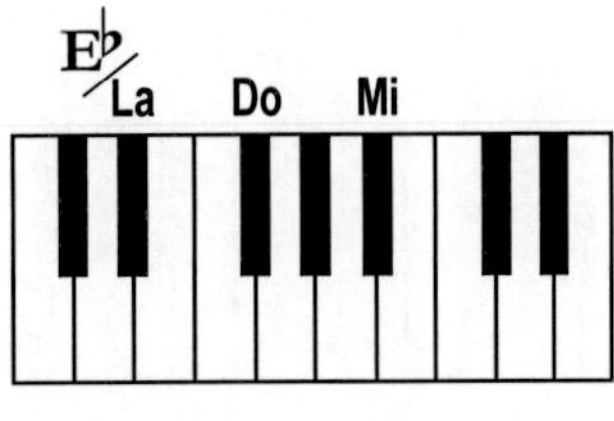

Tonic Minor (i)

Fingers to Use

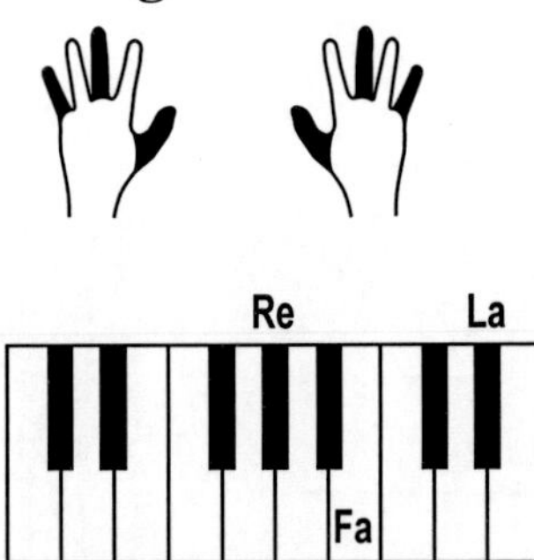

Subdominant Minor (iv)

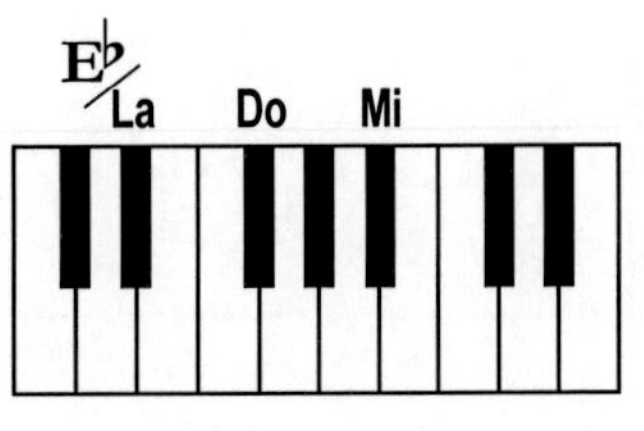

Tonic Minor (i)

Check List

Tonic Arpeggio

Lesson		Home
________	Separated	________
________	Connected	________
________	Sing Syllables	________

Melodic Cadence

Lesson		Home
________	Hand	________
________	Hand	________
________	Separated	________
________	Connected	________
________	Sing Syllables	________
________	Add LH Roots	________

Transposition

Lesson		Home
________	Folk Song	________
________	Folk Song	________
________	Solo	________
________	Solo	________

Major Tonality – When DO is C♭ or B

Tonic Arpeggio

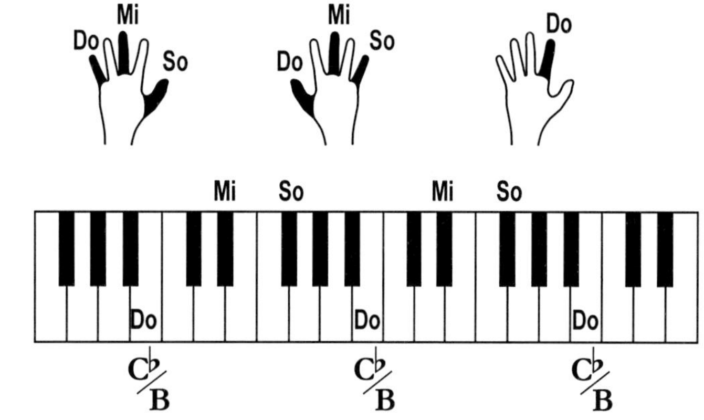

This picture is the keyboard "look" and "feel" of a C♭/B Major arpeggio: W B B

Tonic-Dominant-Tonic Melodic Cadence

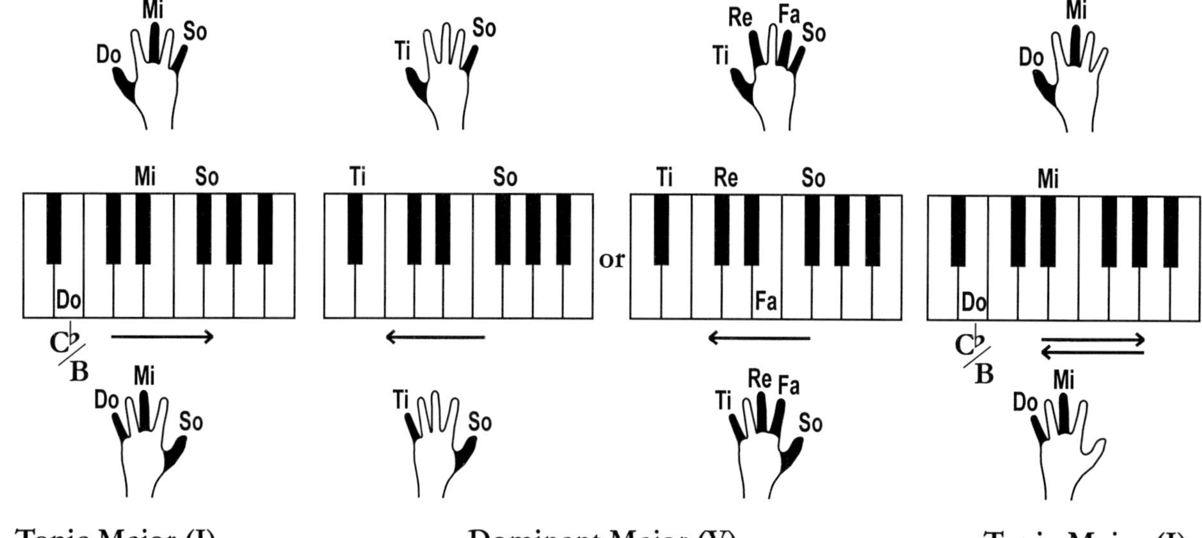

Tonic Major (I) Dominant Major (V) Tonic Major (I)

C♭/B Major Scale

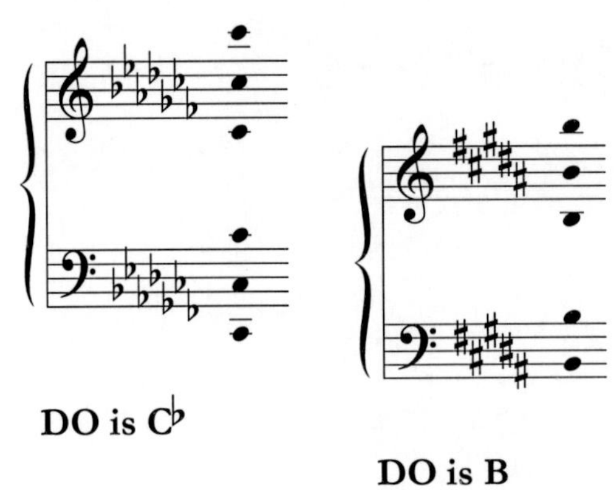

DO is C♭

DO is B

Play the scale with one finger.

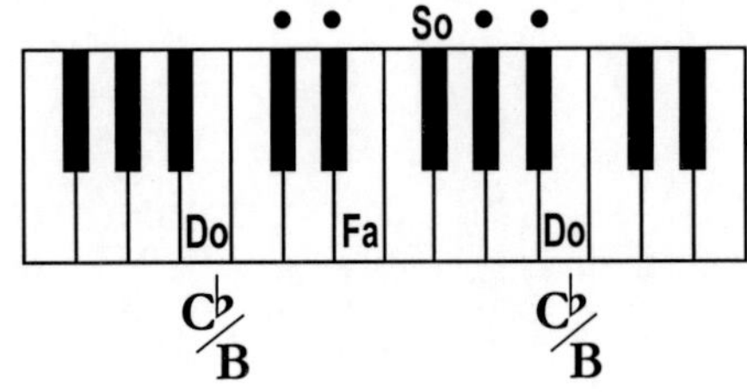

This picture is the keyboard "look" and "feel" of a C♭/B Major scale: W B B W B B B W

Check List

Major Scale

Lesson		Home
________	Hand	________
________	Hand	________
________	Separated	________
________	Connected	________
________	One Octave	________
________	Two Octaves	________
________	Three Octaves	________
________	Four Octaves	________

Learn the thumb crossings.

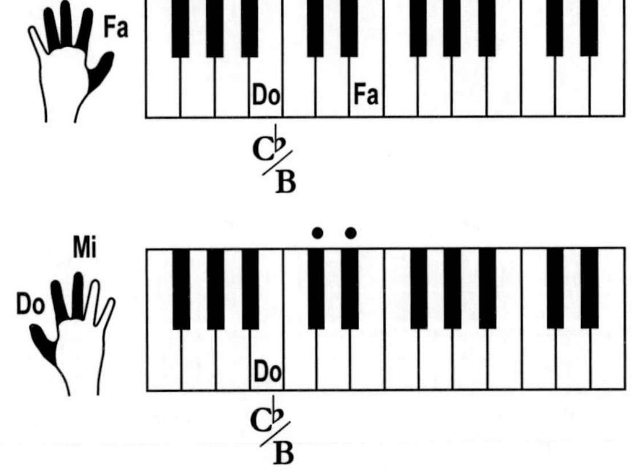

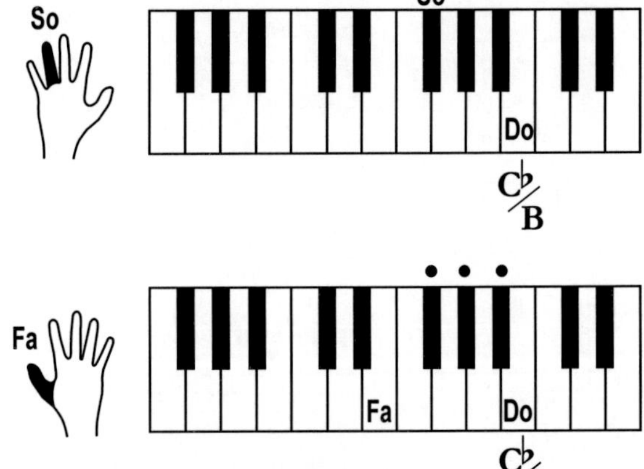

Play the scale from DO to DO.

Harmonic Minor Tonality – When LA is A♭

Check List

Tonic Arpeggio

Lesson		Home
________	Separated	________
________	Connected	________
________	Sing Syllables	________

Melodic Cadence

Lesson		Home
________	Hand	________
________	Hand	________
________	Separated	________
________	Connected	________
________	Sing Syllables	________
________	Add LH Roots	________

Transposition

Lesson		Home
________	Folk Song	________
________	Folk Song	________
________	Solo	________
________	Solo	________

Tonic Arpeggio

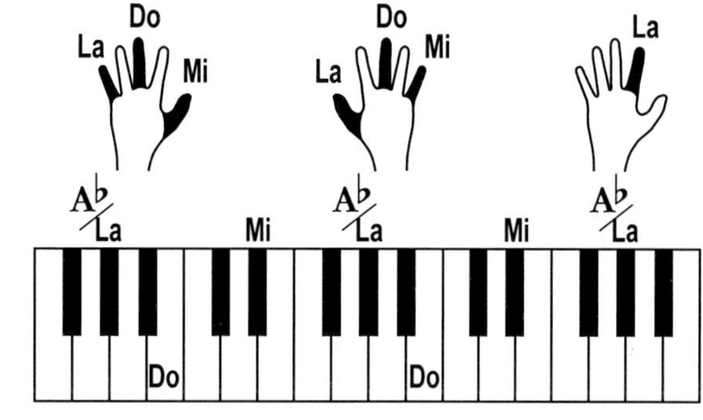

This picture is the keyboard "look" and "feel" of an A♭ Minor arpeggio: B W B.

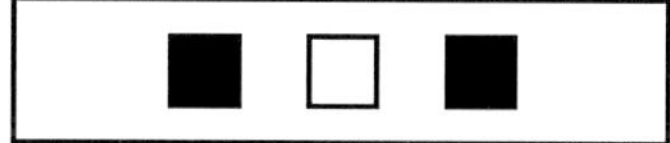

Tonic-Dominant-Tonic Melodic Cadence

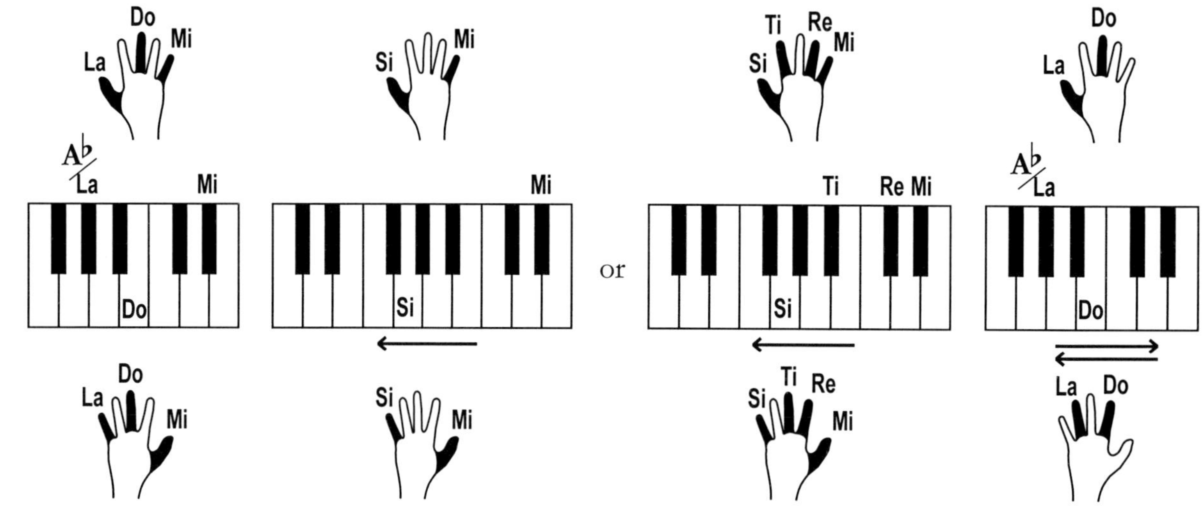

Tonic Minor (i) Dominant Harmonic Minor (V) Tonic Minor (i)

Tonic – Dominant - Tonic Arpeggios
When DO is C♭/B then LA is A♭

Check List

Major Tonality

Lesson		Home
________	Separated	________
________	Connected	________
________	Sing Syllables	________

Harmonic Minor Tonality

Lesson		Home
________	Separated	________
________	Connected	________
________	Sing Syllables	________

When DO is C♭/B then LA is A♭

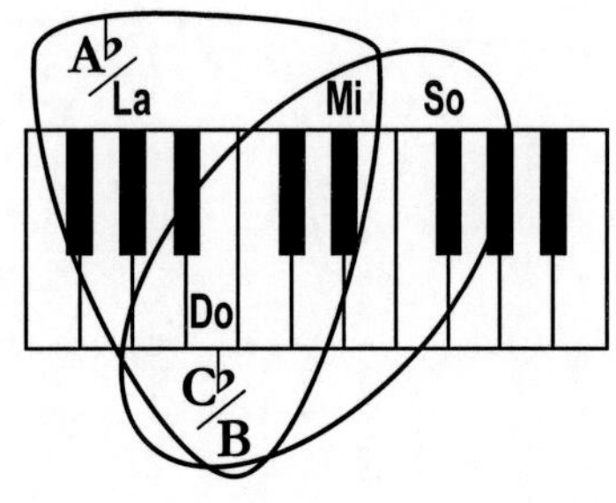

Fingers to Use

Tonic-Dominant-Tonic Arpeggios

Do is C♭/B

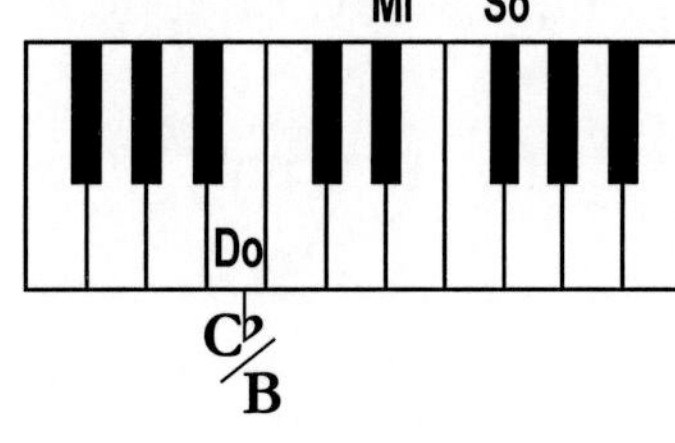

Tonic Major (I)

So Ti Re

Dominant Major (V)

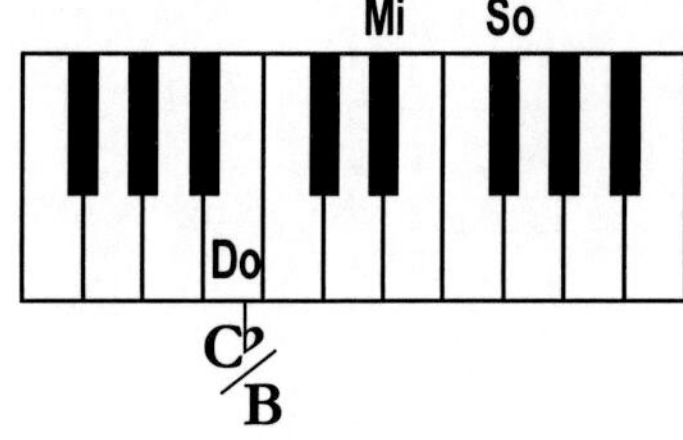

Tonic Major (I)

LA is A♭

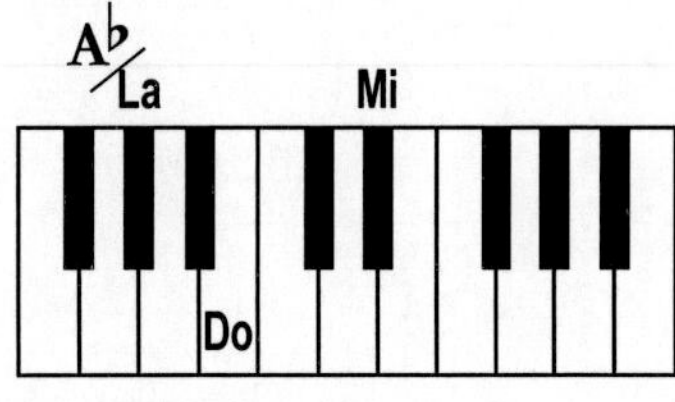

Tonic Minor (i)

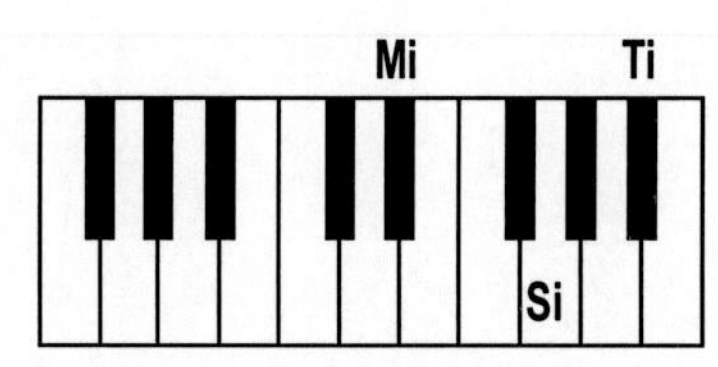

Dominant Harmonic Minor (V)

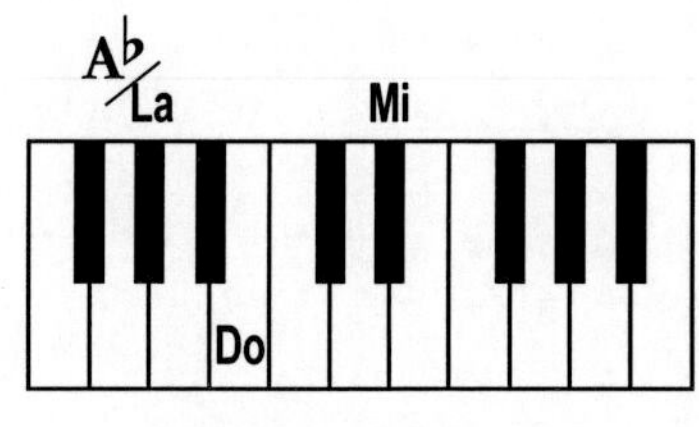

Tonic Minor (i)

Tonic – Subdominant – Tonic
When DO is C♭/B

Check List

Melodic Cadence

Lesson		Home
________	Hand	________
________	Hand	________
________	Separated	________
________	Connected	________
________	Sing Syllables	________
________	Play I-IV-V-I	________
________	Add LH Roots	________

Arpeggios

Lesson		Home
________	Separated	________
________	Connected	________
________	Sing Syllables	________
________	Play I-IV-V-I	________

Melodic Cadence

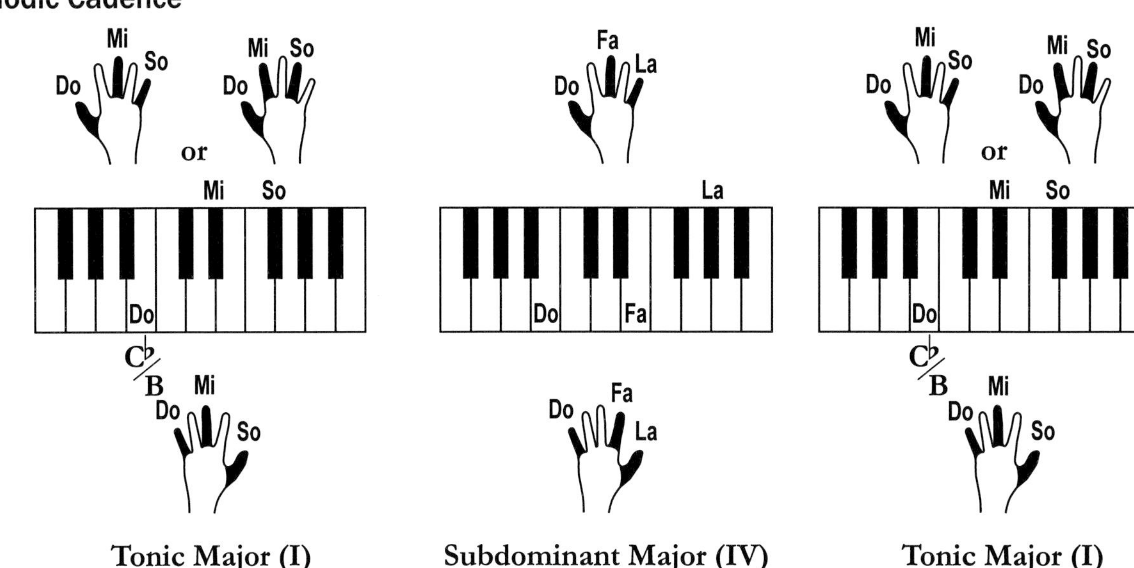

Tonic Major (I) Subdominant Major (IV) Tonic Major (I)

Arpeggios

Fingers to Use

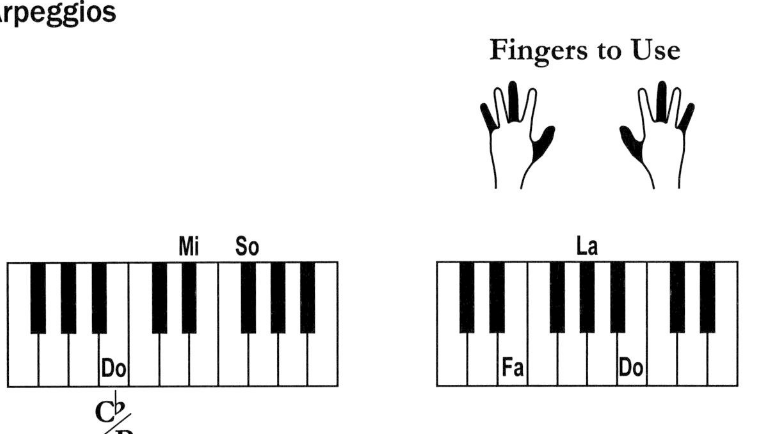

Mi So Do C♭/B

Tonic Major (I) Subdominant Major (IV) Tonic Major (I)

Tonic – Subdominant - Tonic
When LA is A♭

Check List

Melodic Cadence

Lesson		Home
________	Hand	________
________	Hand	________
________	Separated	________
________	Connected	________
________	Sing Syllables	________
________	Play i-iv-V-i	________
________	Add LH Roots	________

Arpeggios

Lesson		Home
________	Separated	________
________	Connected	________
________	Sing Syllables	________
________	Play i-iv-V-i	________

Melodic Cadence

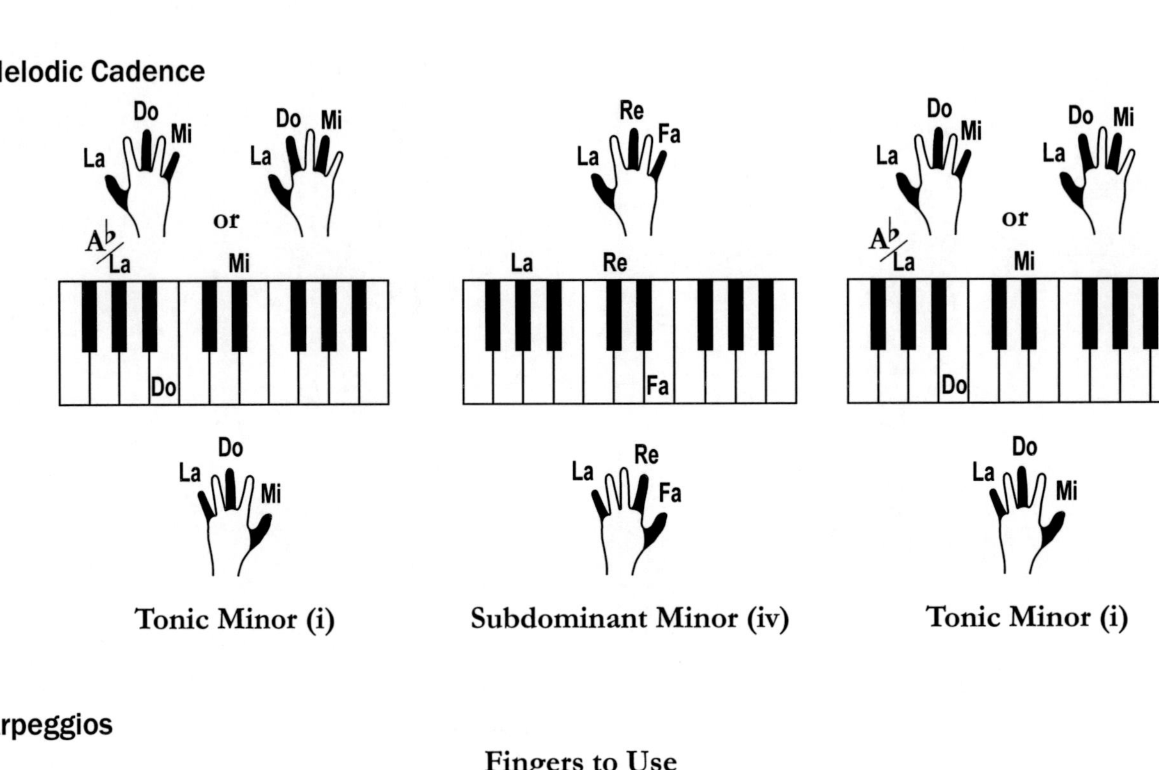

Tonic Minor (i) Subdominant Minor (iv) Tonic Minor (i)

Arpeggios

Fingers to Use

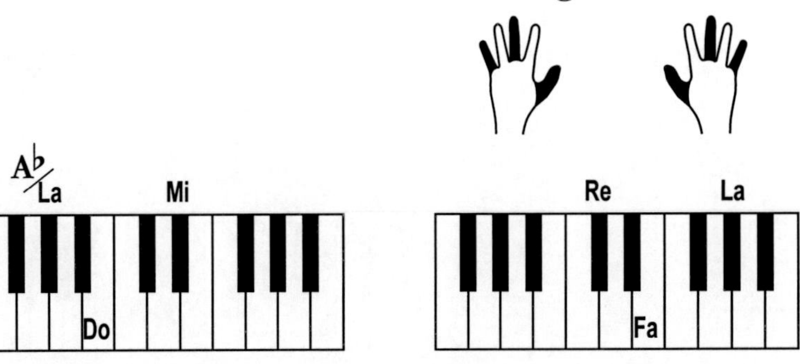

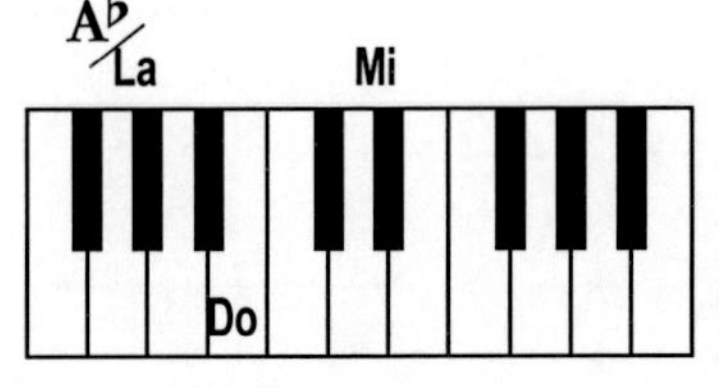

Tonic Minor (i) Subdominant Minor (iv) Tonic Minor (i)

Check List

Tonic Arpeggio

Lesson		Home
________	Separated	________
________	Connected	________
________	Sing Syllables	________

Melodic Cadence

Lesson		Home
________	Hand	________
________	Hand	________
________	Separated	________
________	Connected	________
________	Sing Syllables	________
________	Add LH Roots	________

Transposition

Lesson		Home
________	Folk Song	________
________	Folk Song	________
________	Solo	________
________	Solo	________

Major Tonality - When DO is E

Tonic Arpeggio

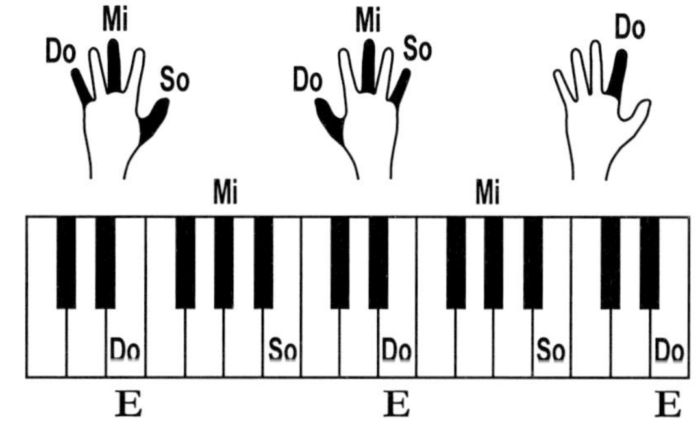

This picture is the keyboard "look" and "feel" of an E Major arpeggio: W B W

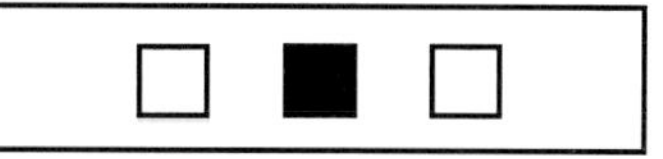

Tonic-Dominant-Tonic Melodic Cadence

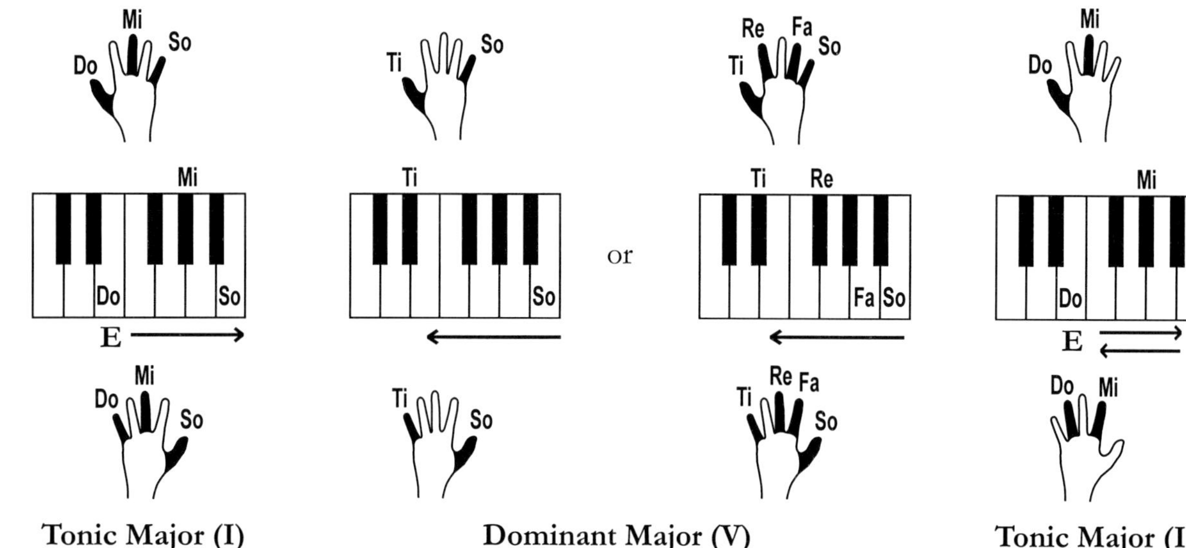

E Major Scale

DO is E

Play the scale with one finger.

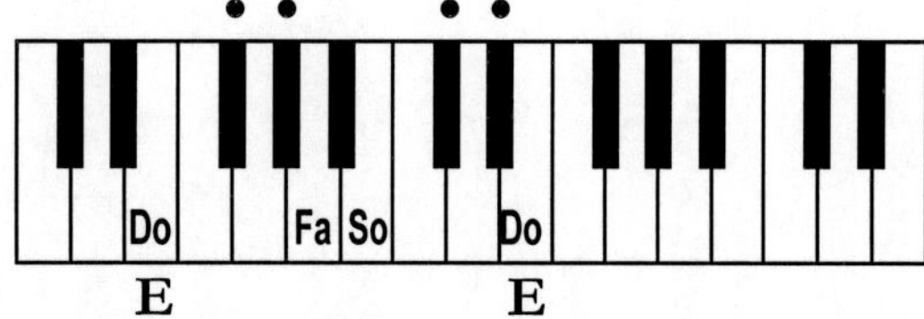

This picture is the keyboard "look" and "feel" of an E Major scale:
W B B W W B BW

Check List

Major Scale

Lesson		Home
________	Hand	________
________	Hand	________
________	Separated	________
________	Connected	________
________	One Octave	________
________	Two Octaves	________
________	Three Octaves	________
________	Four Octaves	________

Learn the thumb crossings.

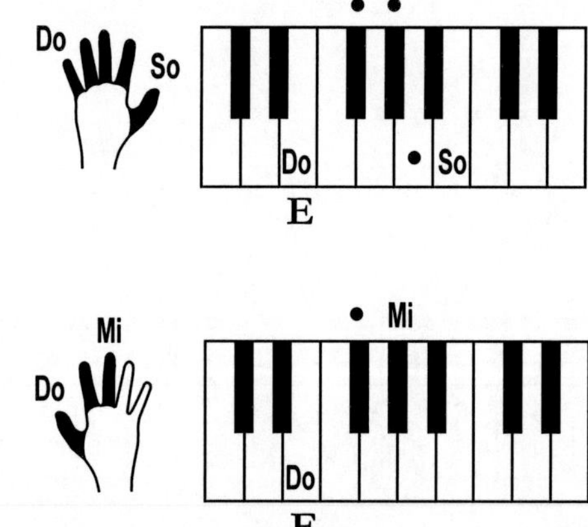

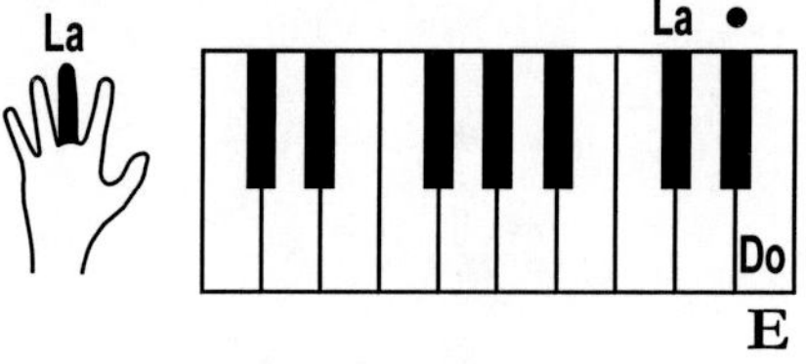

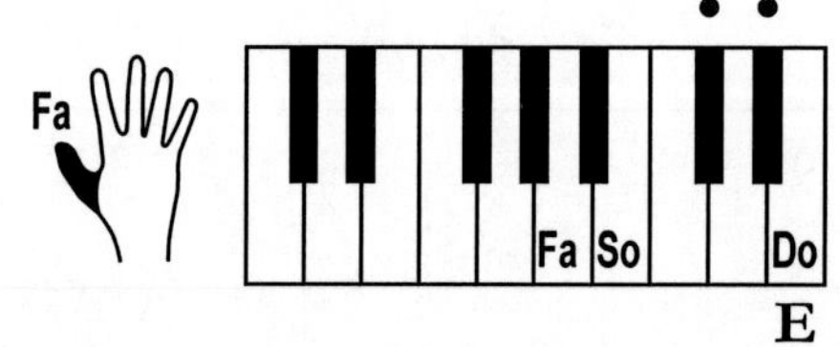

Play the scale from DO to DO.

Harmonic Minor Tonality - When LA is C♯

Check List

Tonic Arpeggio

Lesson		Home
________	Separated	________
________	Connected	________
________	Sing Syllables	________

Melodic Cadence

Lesson		Home
________	Hand (left)	________
________	Hand (right)	________
________	Separated	________
________	Connected	________
________	Sing Syllables	________
________	Add LH Roots	________

Transposition

Lesson		Home
________	Folk Song	________
________	Folk Song	________
________	Solo	________
________	Solo	________

Tonic Arpeggio

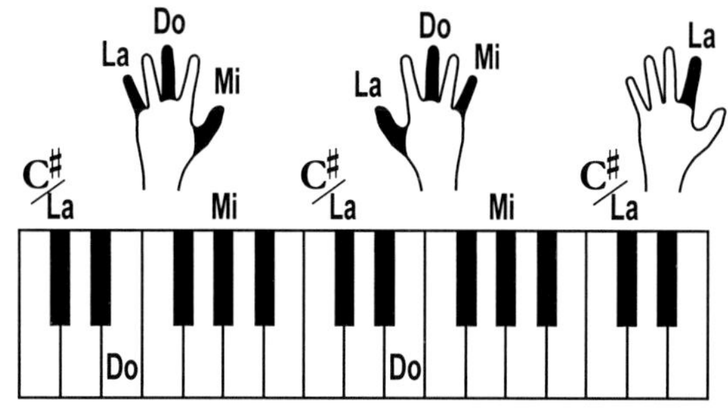

This picture is the keyboard "look" and "feel" of a C♯ Minor arpeggio: B W B

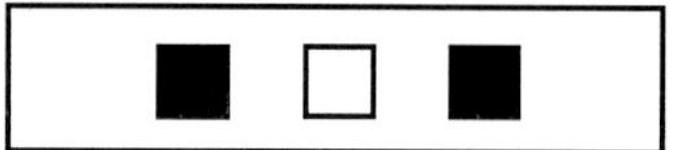

Tonic-Dominant-Tonic Melodic Cadence

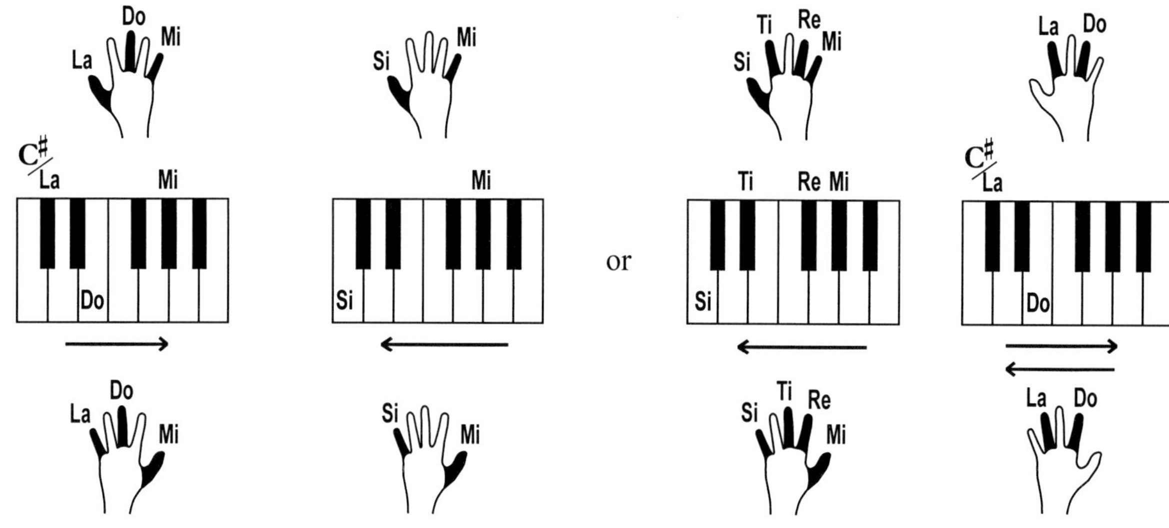

Tonic - Dominant - Tonic Arpeggios
When DO is E then LA is C♯

Check List

Major Tonality

Lesson		Home
________	Separated	________
________	Connected	________
________	Sing Syllables	________

Harmonic Minor Tonality

Lesson		Home
________	Separated	________
________	Connected	________
________	Sing Syllables	________

When DO is E then LA is C♯

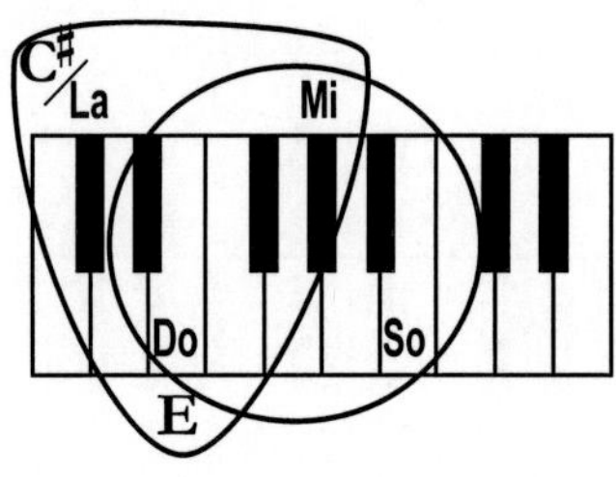

Fingers to Use

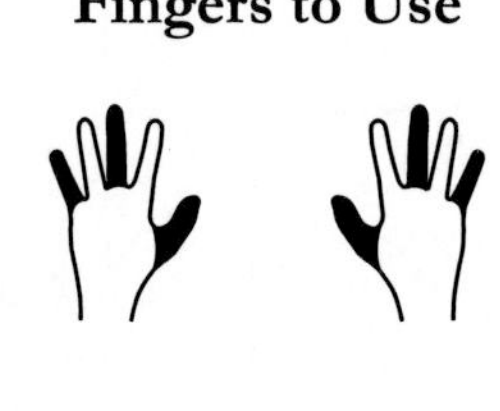

Tonic-Dominant-Tonic Arpeggios

DO is E

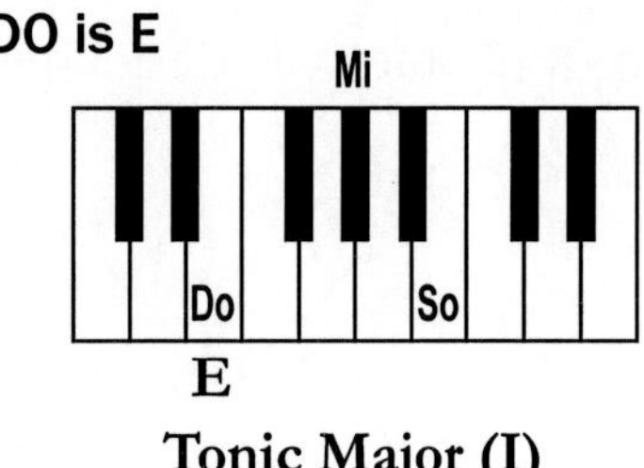

Tonic Major (I)

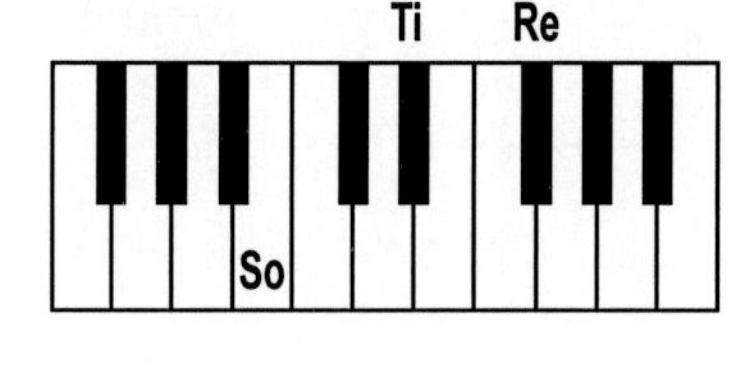

Dominant Major (V)

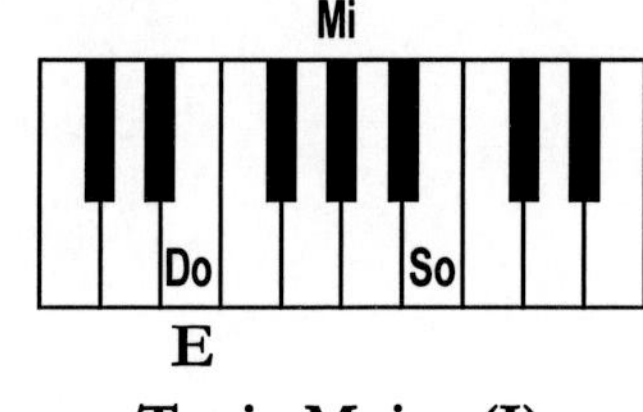

Tonic Major (I)

LA is C♯

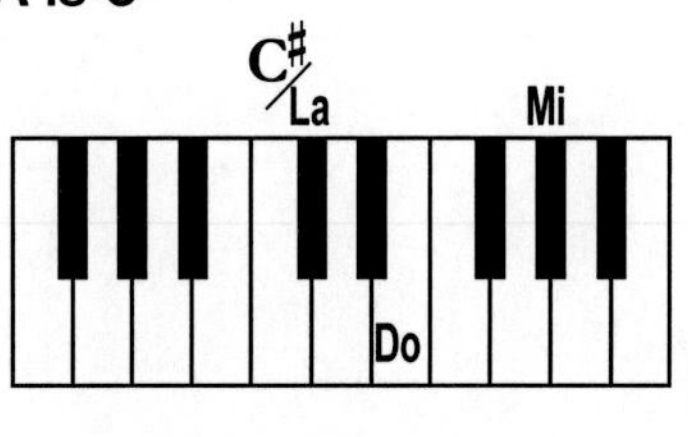

Tonic Minor (i)

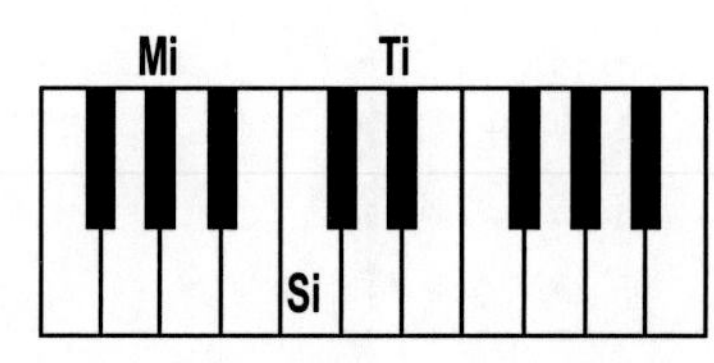

Dominant Harmonic Minor (V)

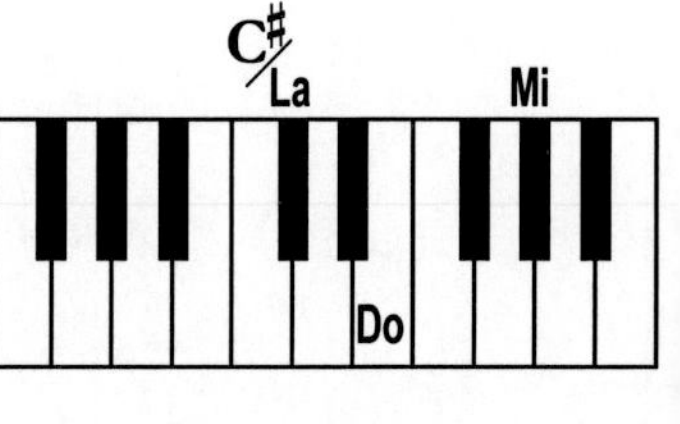

Tonic Minor (i)

Tonic - Subdominant - Tonic
When DO is E

Check List

Melodic Cadence

Lesson		Home
______	Hand	______
______	Hand	______
______	Separated	______
______	Connected	______
______	Sing Syllables	______
______	Play I-IV-V-I	______
______	Add LH Roots	______

Arpeggios

Lesson		Home
______	Separated	______
______	Connected	______
______	Sing Syllables	______
______	Play I-IV-V-I	______

Melodic Cadence

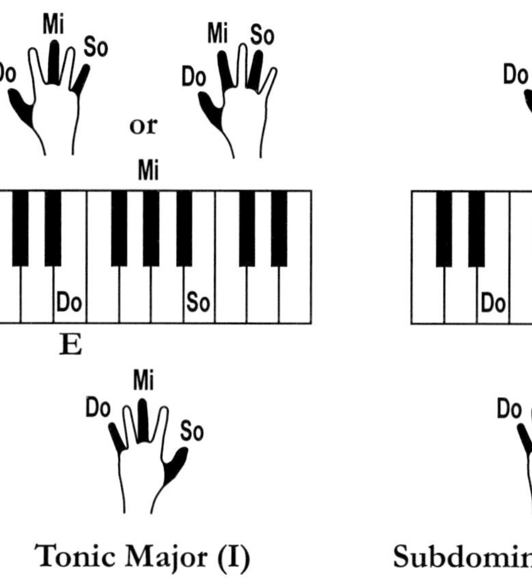

Tonic Major (I)

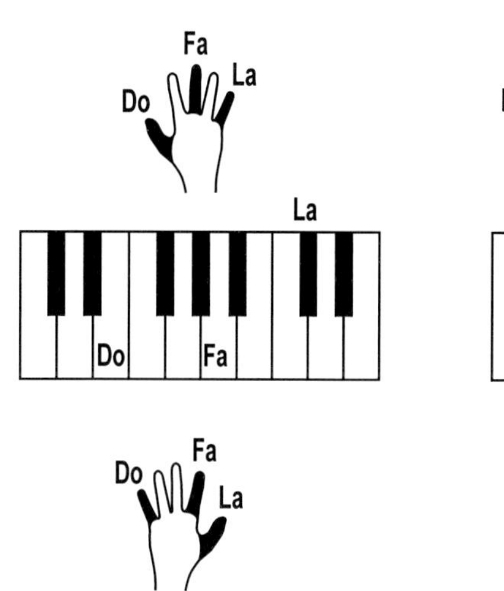

Subdominant Major (IV)

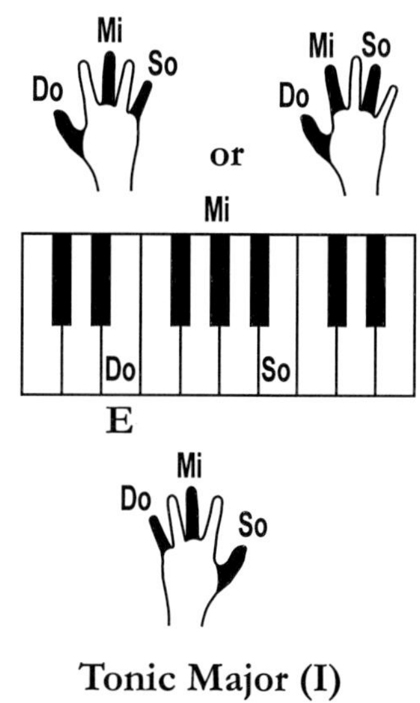

Tonic Major (I)

Arpeggios

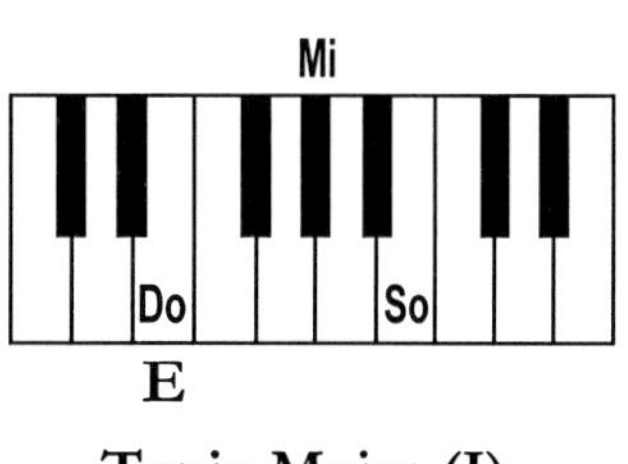

Tonic Major (I)

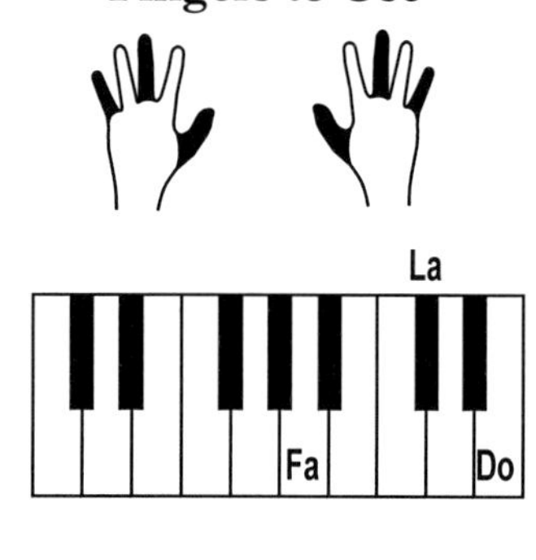

Subdominant Major (IV)

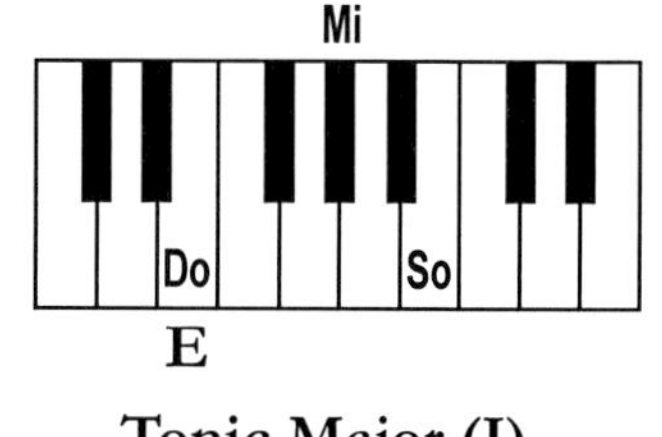

Tonic Major (I)

Tonic - Subdominant - Tonic
When LA is C♯

Check List

Melodic Cadence

Lesson		Home
________	Hand	________
________	Hand	________
________	Separated	________
________	Connected	________
________	Sing Syllables	________
________	Play i-iv-V-i	________
________	Add LH Roots	________

Arpeggios

Lesson		Home
________	Separated	________
________	Connected	________
________	Sing Syllables	________
________	Play i-iv-V-i	________

Melodic Cadence

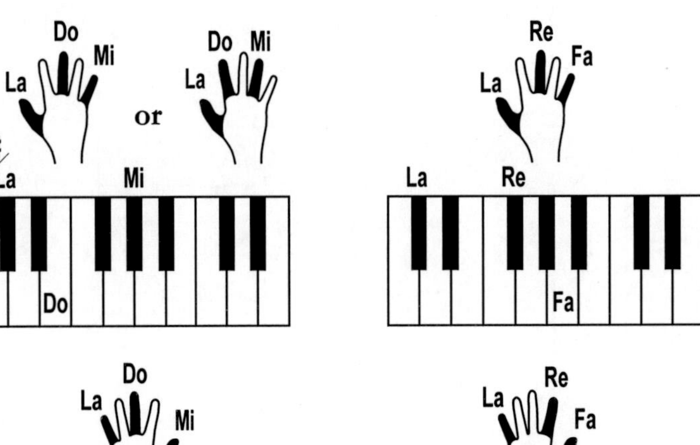

Do
Mi
La
or
Do Mi
La
C♯
La
Mi
Do
La
Do
Mi

Tonic Minor (i) | Subdominant Minor (iv) | Tonic Minor (i)

Arpeggios

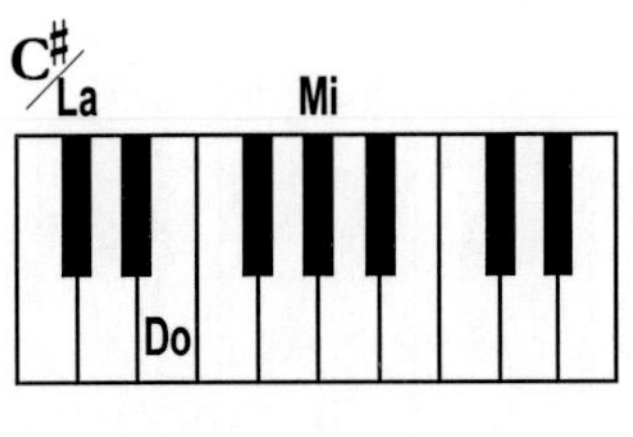

Tonic Minor (i)

Fingers to Use

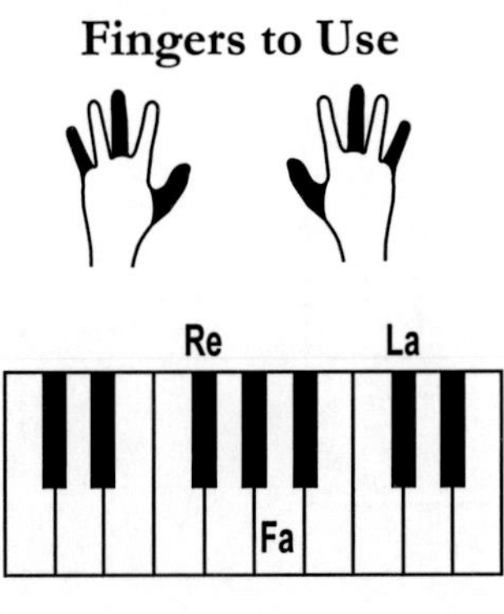

Subdominant Minor (iv)

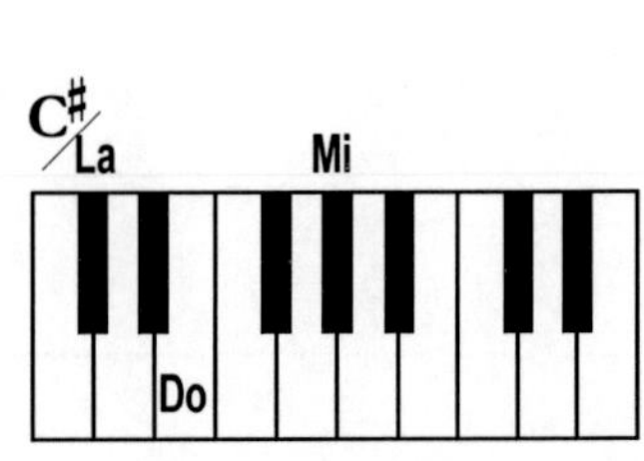

Tonic Minor (i)

Check List

Tonic Arpeggio

Lesson		Home
________	Separated	________
________	Connected	________
________	Sing Syllables	________

Melodic Cadence

Lesson		Home
________	Hand	________
________	Hand	________
________	Separated	________
________	Connected	________
________	Sing Syllables	________
________	Add LH Roots	________

Transposition

Lesson		Home
________	Folk Song	________
________	Folk Song	________
________	Solo	________
________	Solo	________

Major Tonality – When DO is A

Tonic Arpeggio

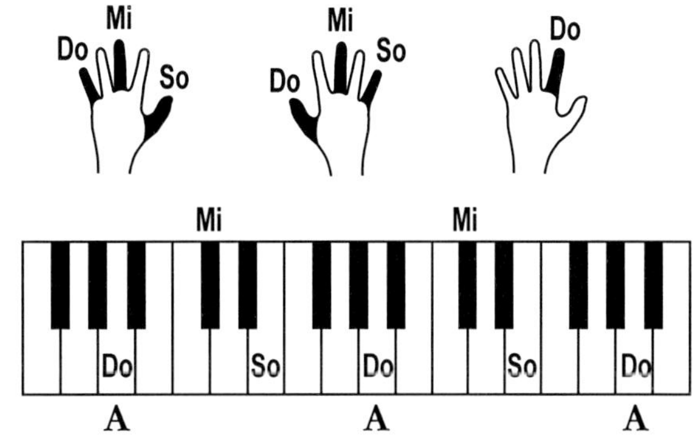

This picture is the keyboard "look" and "feel" of an A Major arpeggio: W B W

Tonic-Dominant-Tonic Melodic Cadence

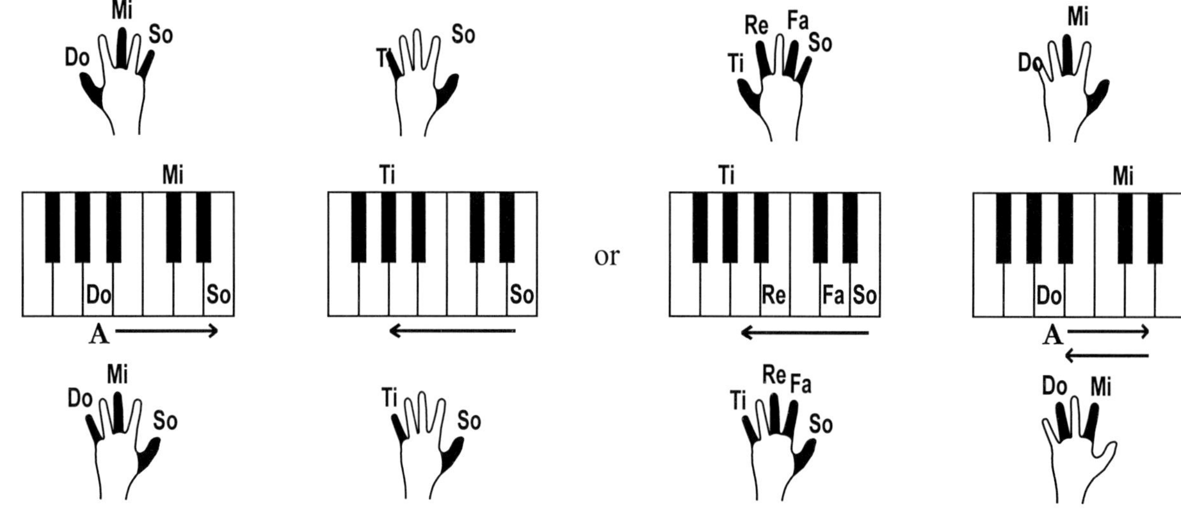

Tonic Major (I) Dominant Major (V) Tonic Major (I)

A Major Scale

DO is A

Check List

Major Scale

Lesson		Home
________	Hand	________
________	Hand	________
________	Separated	________
________	Connected	________
________	One Octave	________
________	Two Octaves	________
________	Three Octaves	________
________	Four Octaves	________

Play the scale with one finger.

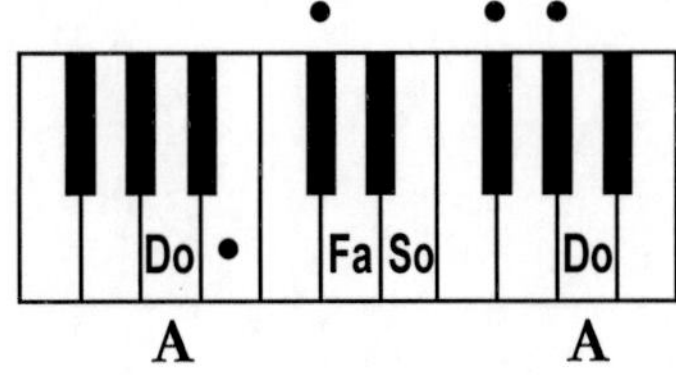

This picture is the keyboard "look" and "feel" of an A Major scale:
W W B W W B B W

Learn the thumb crossings.

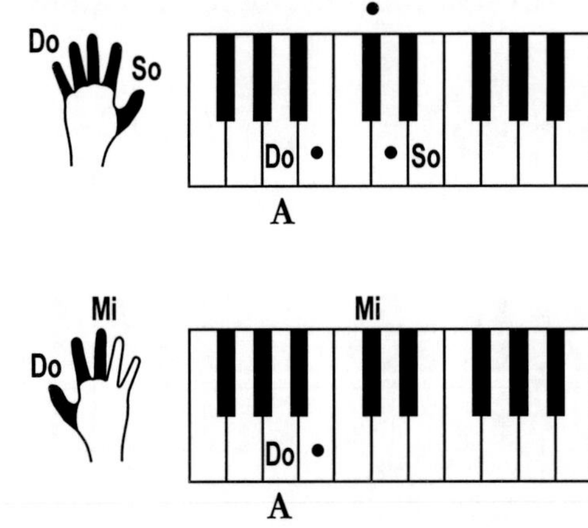

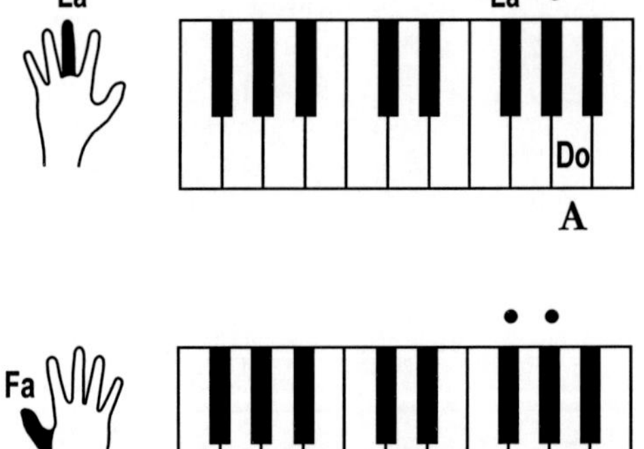

Play the scale from DO to DO.

Harmonic Minor Tonality – When LA is F♯

Check List

Tonic Arpeggio

Lesson		Home
________	Separated	________
________	Connected	________
________	Sing Syllables	________

Melodic Cadence

Lesson		Home
________	Hand	________
________	Hand	________
________	Separated	________
________	Connected	________
________	Sing Syllables	________
________	Add LH Roots	________

Transposition

Lesson		Home
________	Folk Song	________
________	Folk Song	________
________	Solo	________
________	Solo	________

Tonic Arpeggio

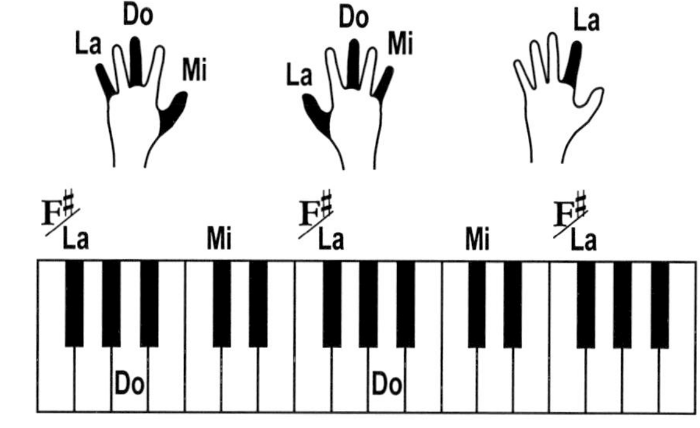

This picture is the keyboard "look" and "feel" of an F♯ Minor arpeggio: B W B

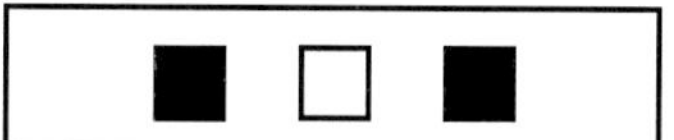

Tonic-Dominant-Tonic Melodic Cadence

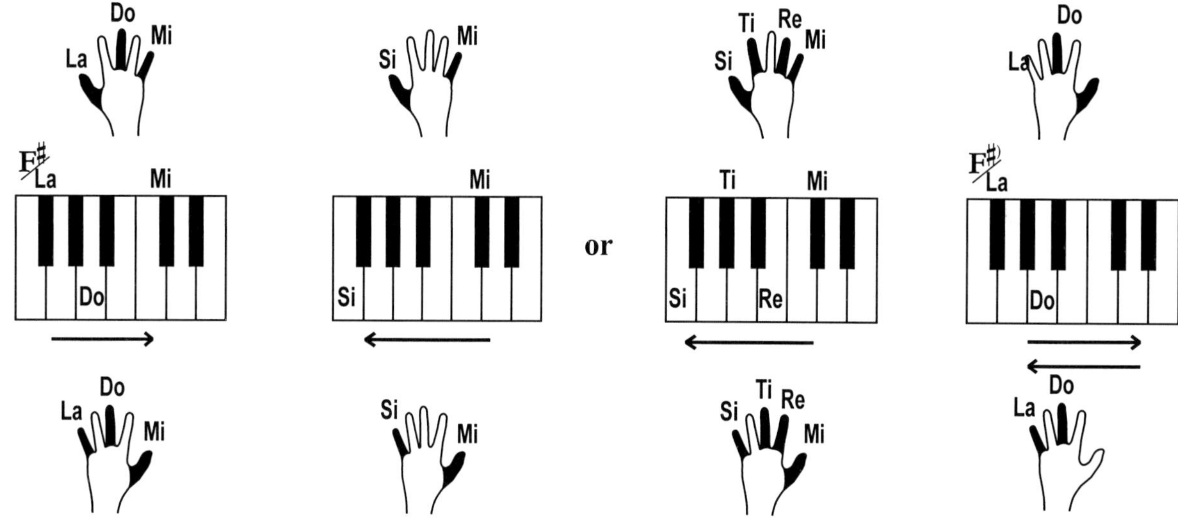

Tonic - Dominant - Tonic Arpeggios
When DO is A then LA is F♯

Check List

Major Tonality

Lesson		Home
________	Separated	________
________	Connected	________
________	Sing Syllables	________

Harmonic Minor Tonality

Lesson		Home
________	Separated	________
________	Connected	________
________	Sing Syllables	________

When DO is A then LA is F♯

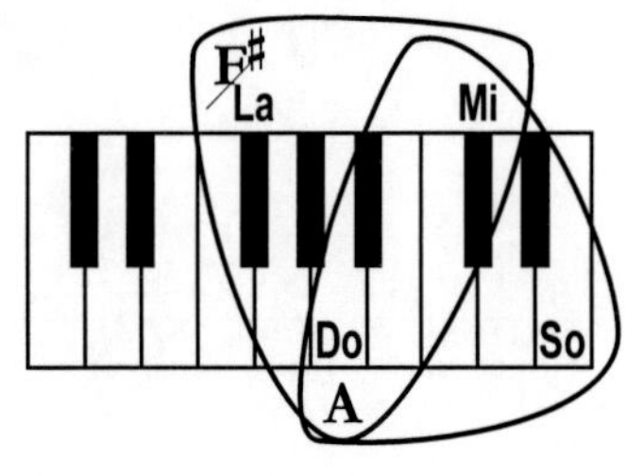

Fingers to use

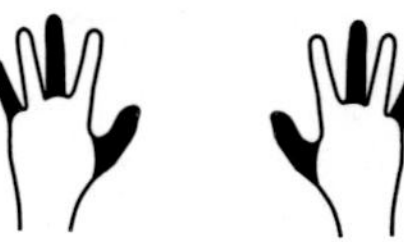

Tonic-Dominant-Tonic Arpeggios

DO is A

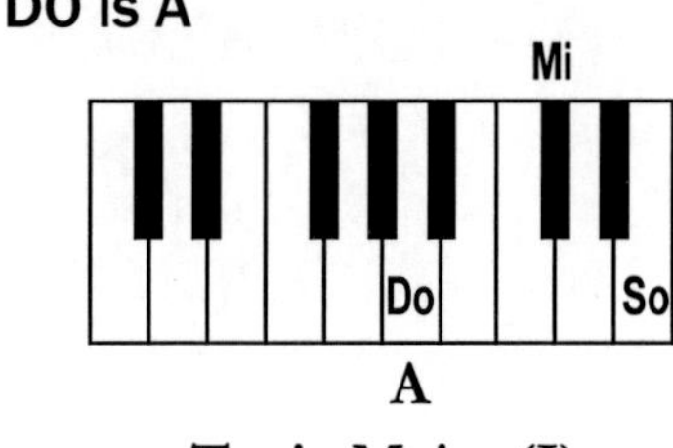

Tonic Major (I)

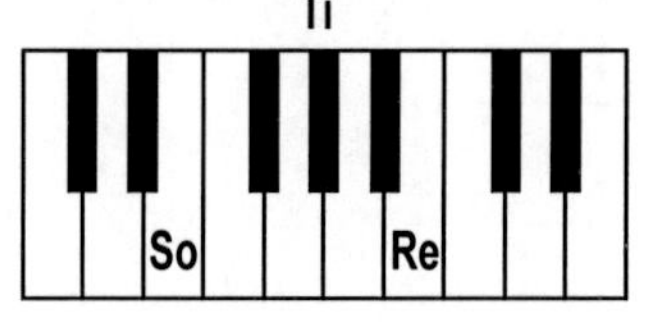

Dominant Major (V)

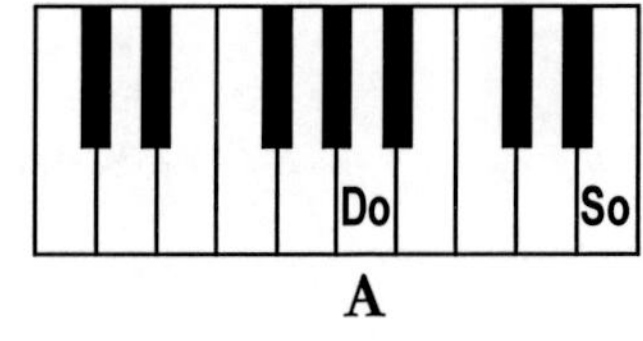

Tonic Major (I)

LA is F♯

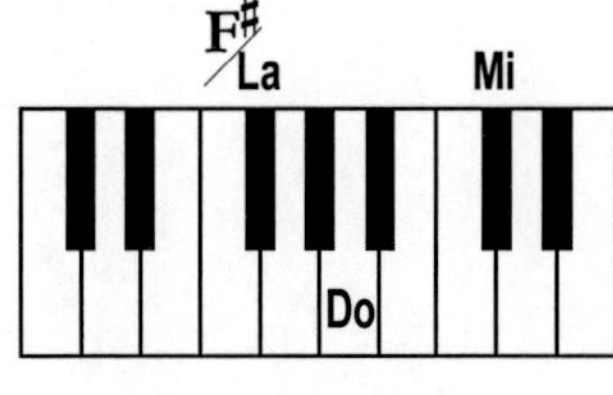

Tonic Minor (i)

Mi Ti

Si

Dominant Harmonic Minor (V)

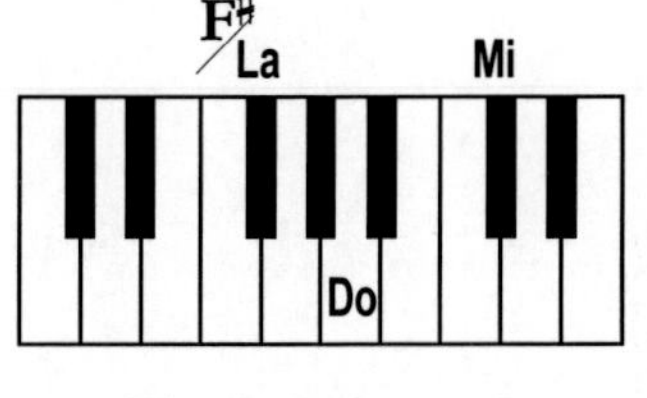

Tonic Minor (i)

Tonic - Subdominant - Tonic
When DO is A

Check List

Melodic Cadence

Lesson		Home
________	Hand 	________
________	Hand	________
________	Separated	________
________	Connected	________
________	Sing Syllables	________
________	Play I-IV-V-I	________
________	Add LH Roots	________

Arpeggios

Lesson		Home
________	Separated	________
________	Connected	________
________	Sing Syllables	________
________	Play I-IV-V-I	________

Melodic Cadence

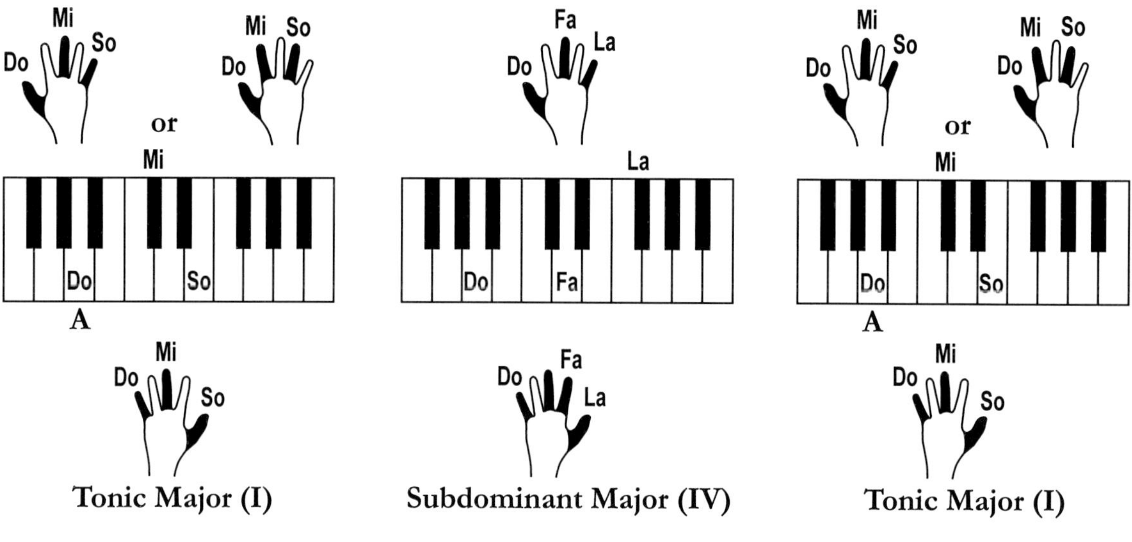

Tonic Major (I) Subdominant Major (IV) Tonic Major (I)

Arpeggios

Fingers to Use

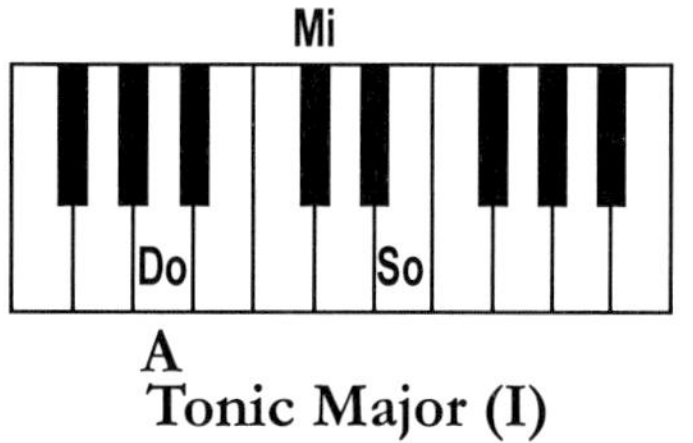

Tonic Major (I)

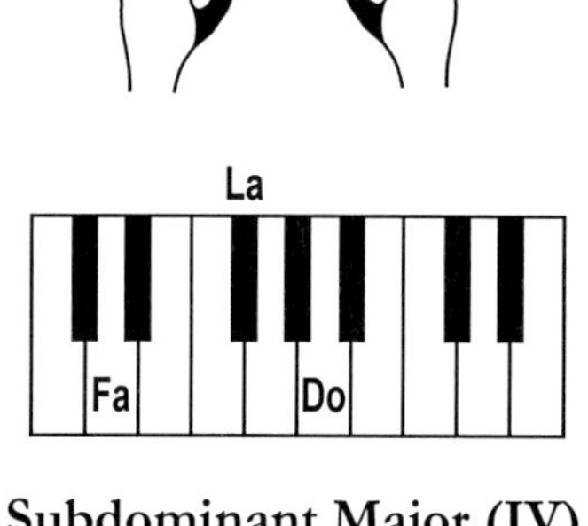

Subdominant Major (IV)

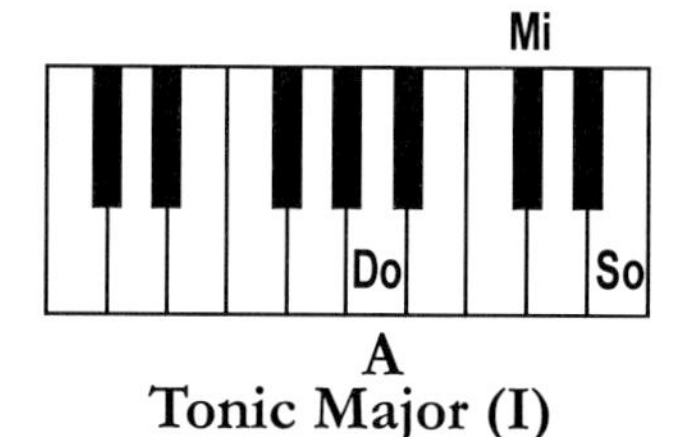

Tonic Major (I)

Tonic - Subdominant - Tonic
When LA is F♯

Check List

Melodic Cadence

Lesson		Home
______	Hand	______
______	Hand	______
______	Separated	______
______	Connected	______
______	Sing Syllables	______
______	Play i-iv-V-i	______
______	Add LH Roots	______

Arpeggios

Lesson		Home
______	Separated	______
______	Connected	______
______	Sing Syllables	______
______	Play i-iv-V-i	______

Melodic Cadence

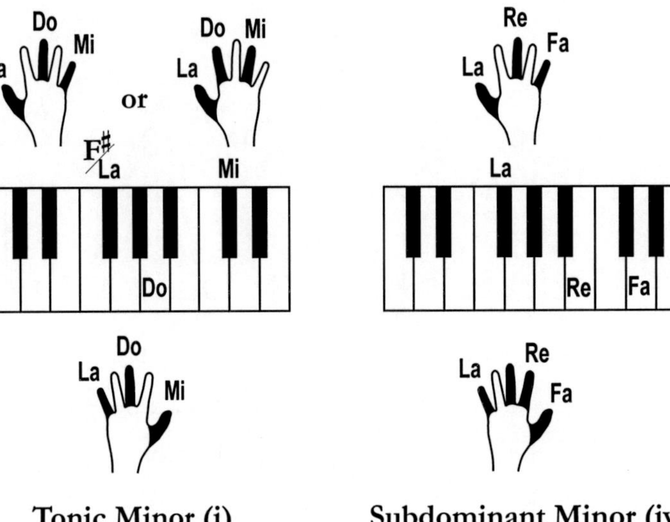

Tonic Minor (i)

Subdominant Minor (iv)

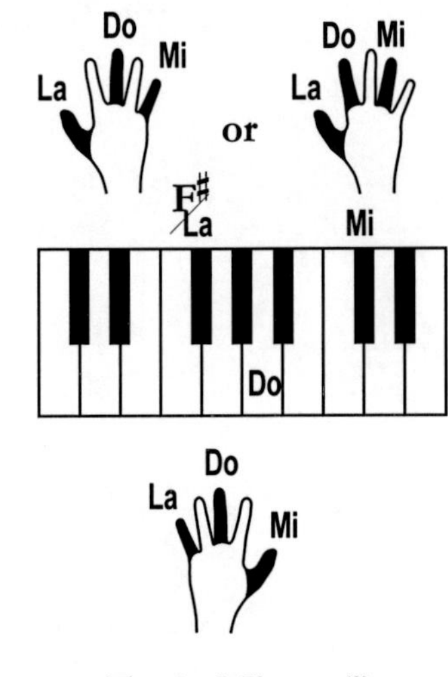

Tonic Minor (i)

Arpeggios

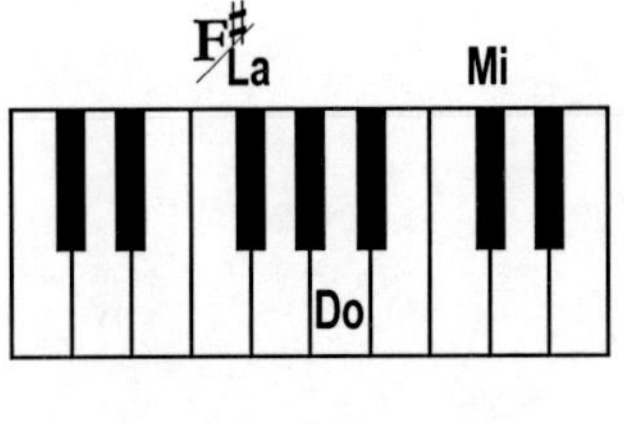

Tonic Minor (i)

Fingers to Use

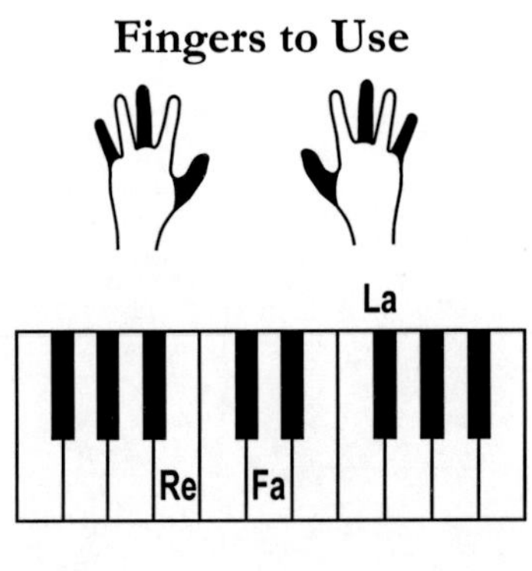

Subdominant Minor (iv)

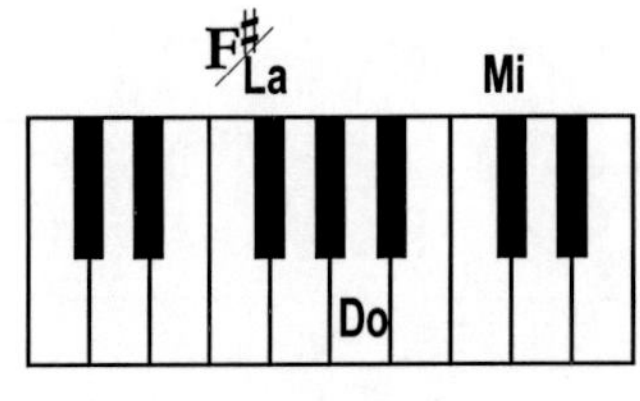

Tonic Minor (i)

Check List

Tonic Arpeggio

Lesson		Home
________	Separated	________
________	Connected	________
________	Sing Syllables	________

Melodic Cadence

Lesson		Home
________	Hand	________
________	Hand	________
________	Separated	________
________	Connected	________
________	Sing Syllables	________
________	Add LH Roots	________

Transposition

Lesson		Home
________	Folk Song	________
________	Folk Song	________
________	Solo	________
________	Solo	________

Major Tonality - When DO is D

Tonic Arpeggio

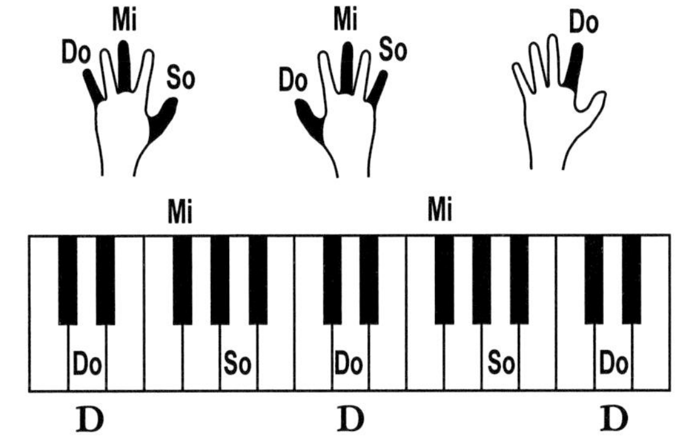

This picture is the keyboard "look" and "feel" of a D Major arpeggio: W B W

Tonic-Dominant-Tonic Melodic Cadence

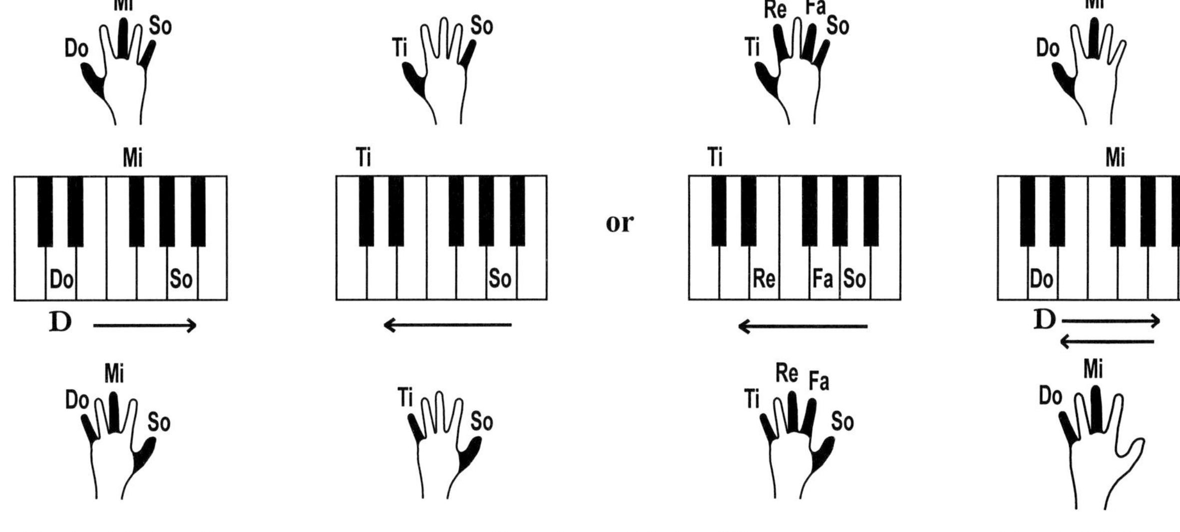

D Major Scale

DO is D

Play the scale with one finger.

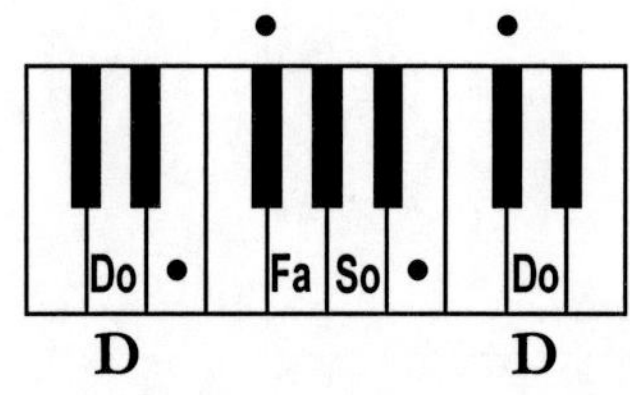

This picture is the keyboard "look" and "feel" of a D Major scale:
W W B W W W B W

Check List

Major Scale

Lesson		Home
________	Hand	________
________	Hand	________
________	Separated	________
________	Connected	________
________	One Octave	________
________	Two Octaves	________
________	Three Octaves	________
________	Four Octaves	________

Learn the thumb crossings.

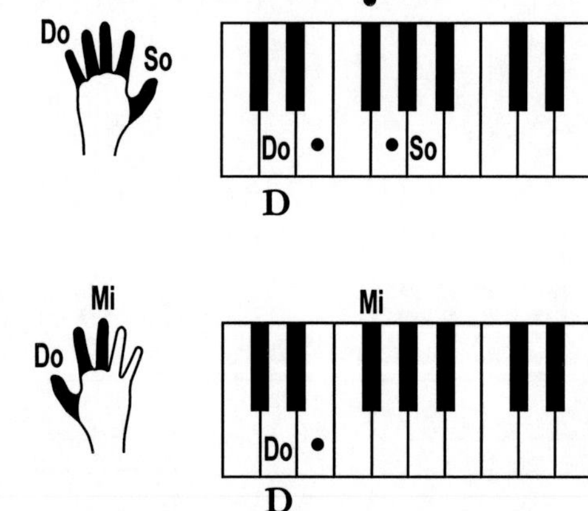

La

La
Do
D

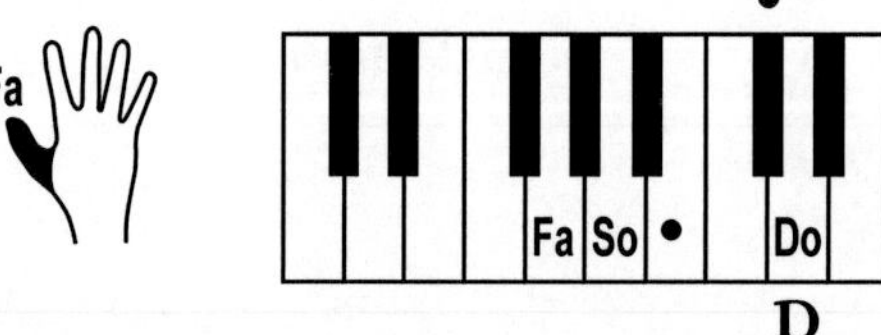

Play the scale from DO to DO.

Check List

Tonic Arpeggio

Lesson		Home
______	Separated	______
______	Connected	______
______	Sing Syllables	______

Melodic Cadence

Lesson		Home
______	Hand	______
______	Hand	______
______	Separated	______
______	Connected	______
______	Sing Syllables	______
______	Add LH Roots	______

Transposition

Lesson		Home
______	Folk Song	______
______	Folk Song	______
______	Solo	______
______	Solo	______

Harmonic Minor Tonality – When LA is B

Tonic Arpeggio

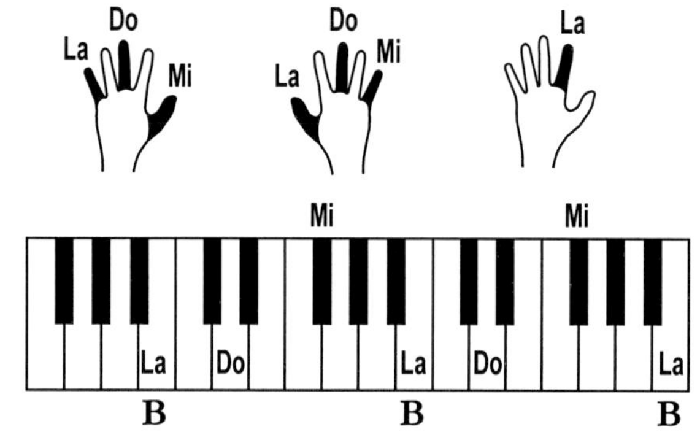

This picture is the keyboard "look" and "feel" of a B Minor arpeggio: W W B

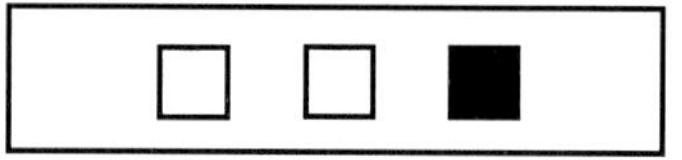

Tonic-Dominant-Tonic Melodic Cadence

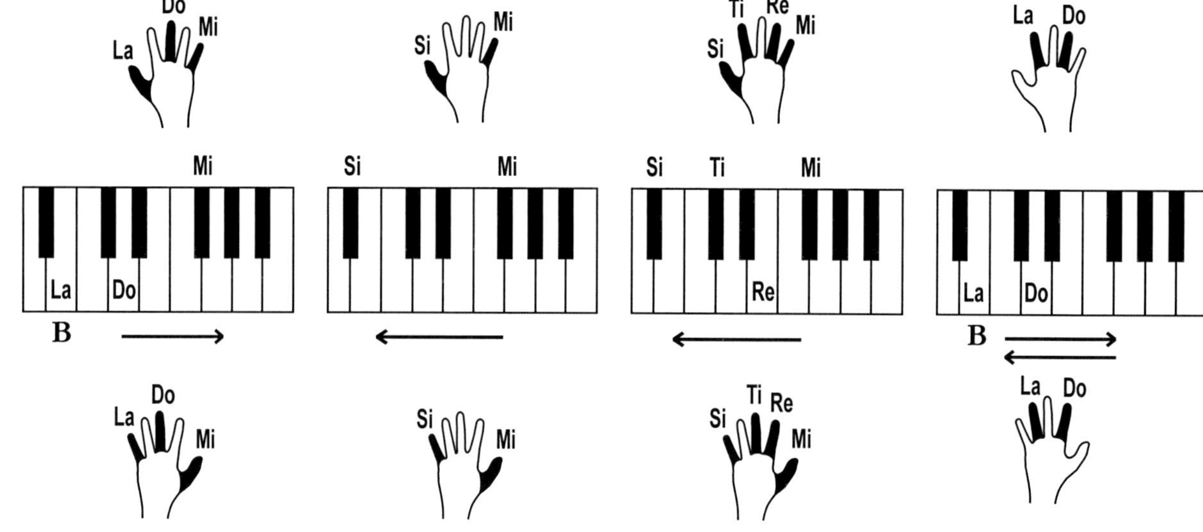

Tonic Minor (i) Dominant Harmonic Minor (V) Tonic Minor (i)

Tonic - Dominant - Tonic Arpeggios
When DO is D then LA is B

Check List

Major Tonality

Lesson		Home
______	Separated	______
______	Connected	______
______	Sing Syllables	______

Harmonic Minor Tonality

Lesson		Home
______	Separated	______
______	Connected	______
______	Sing Syllables	______

When DO is D then LA is B

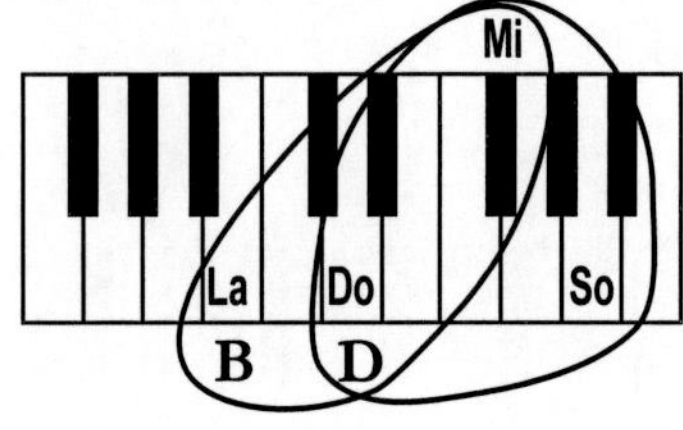

Fingers to Use

Tonic-Dominant-Tonic Arpeggios

DO is D

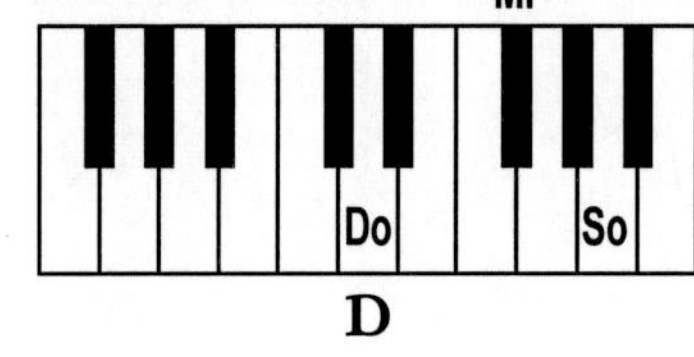

Tonic Major (I)

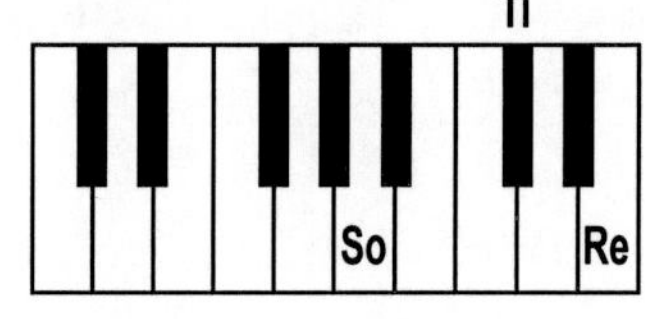

Dominant Major (V)

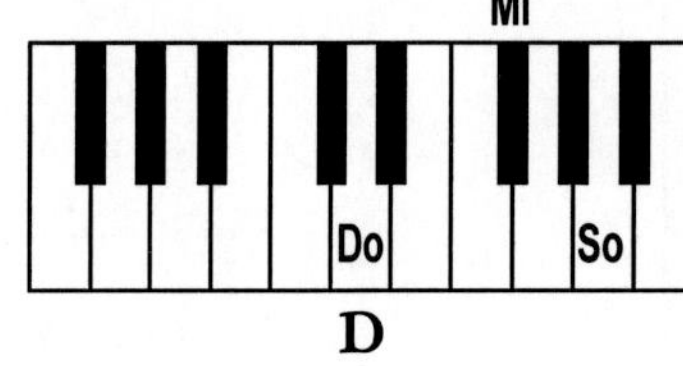

Tonic Major (I)

LA is B

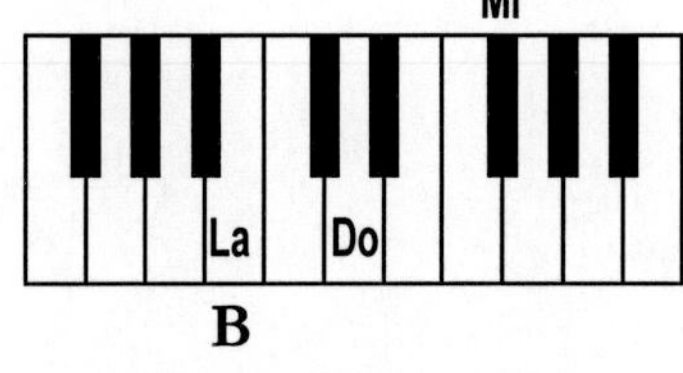

Tonic Minor (i)

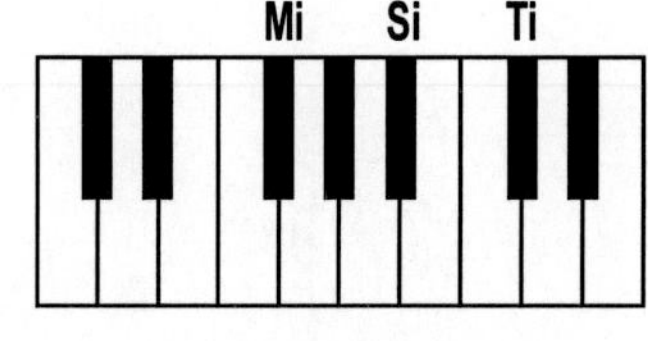

Dominant Harmonic Minor (V)

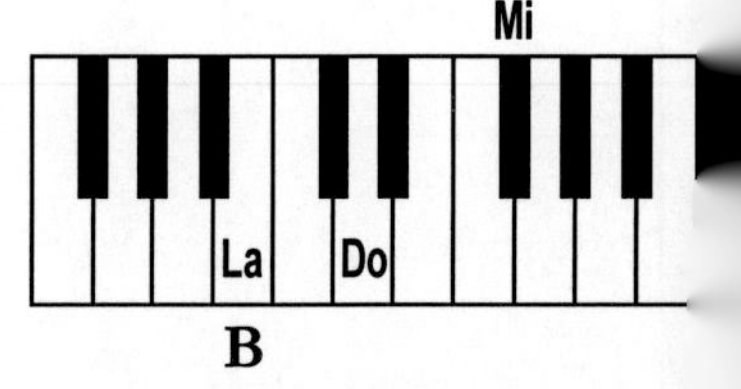

Tonic Minor (i)

Tonic - Subdominant - Tonic
When DO is D

Check List

Melodic Cadence

Lesson		Home
________	Hand	________
________	Hand	________
________	Separated	________
________	Connected	________
________	Sing Syllables	________
________	Play I-IV-V-I	________
________	Add LH Roots	________

Arpeggios

Lesson		Home
________	Separated	________
________	Connected	________
________	Sing Syllables	________
________	Play I-IV-V-I	________

Melodic Cadence

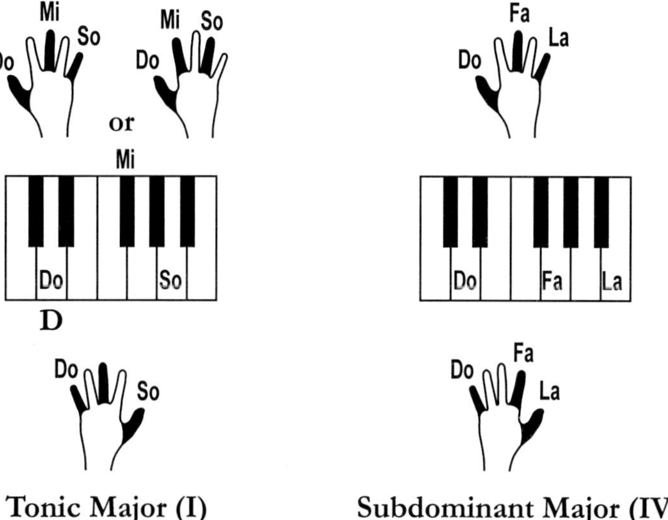

Tonic Major (I)

Subdominant Major (IV)

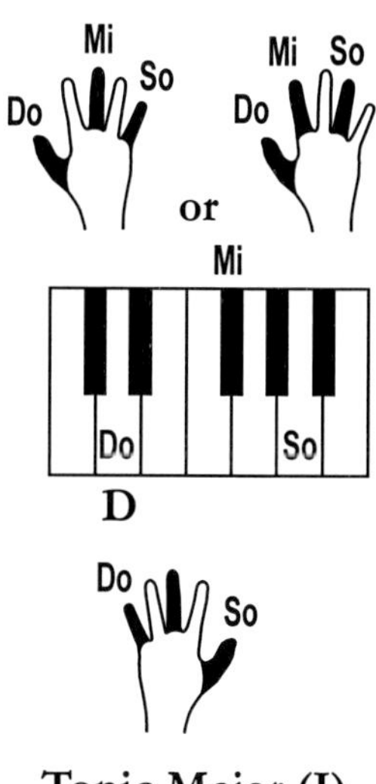

Tonic Major (I)

Arpeggios

Fingers to Use

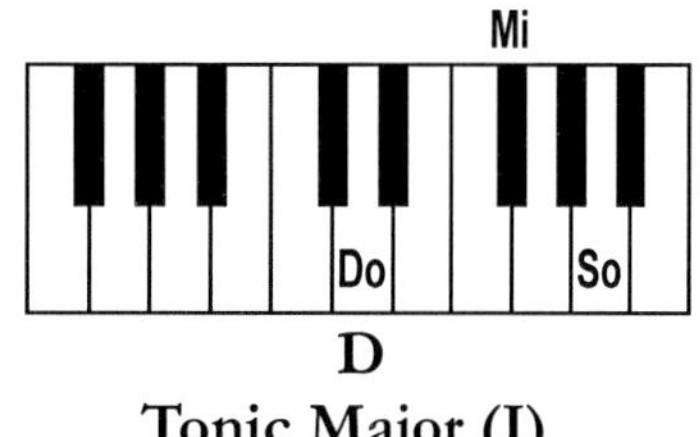

Tonic Major (I)

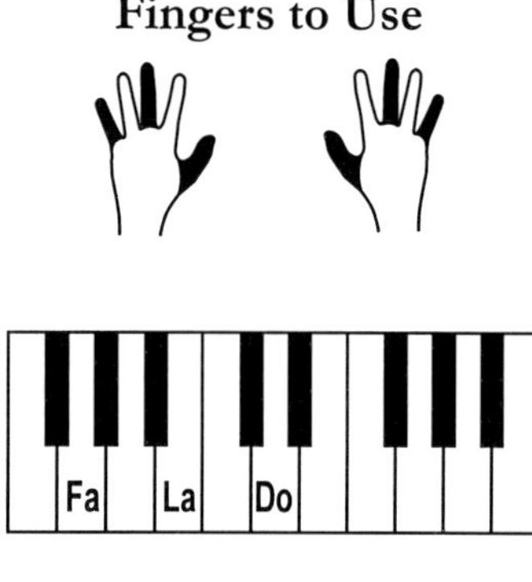

Subdominant Major (IV)

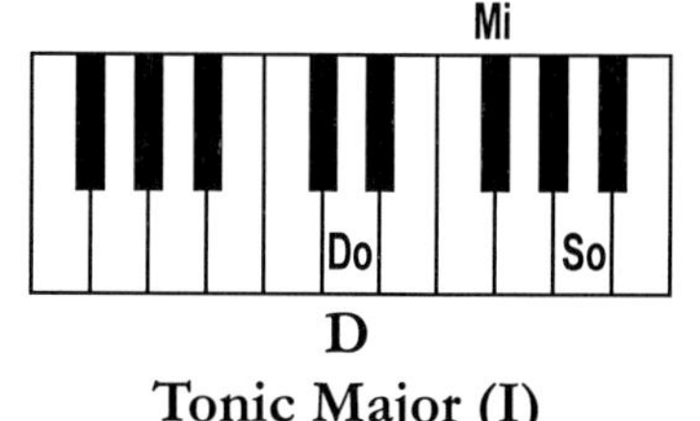

Tonic Major (I)

Tonic - Subdominant - Tonic
When LA is B

Check List

Melodic Cadence

Lesson		Home
________	Hand	________
________	Hand	________
________	Separated	________
________	Connected	________
________	Sing Syllables	________
________	Play i-iv-V-i	________
________	Add LH Roots	________

Arpeggios

Lesson		Home
________	Separated	________
________	Connected	________
________	Sing Syllables	________
________	Play i-iv-V-i	________

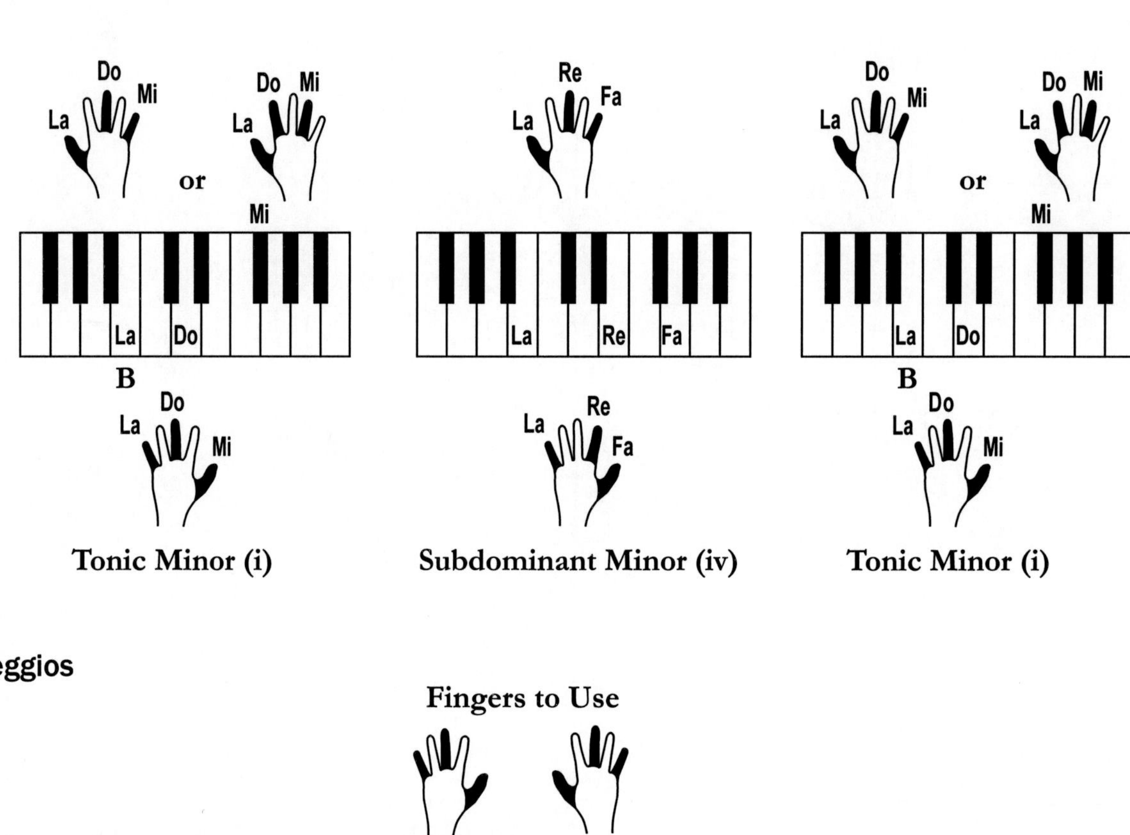

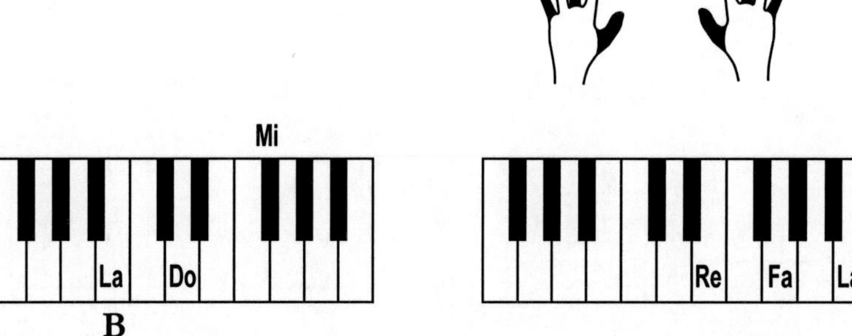

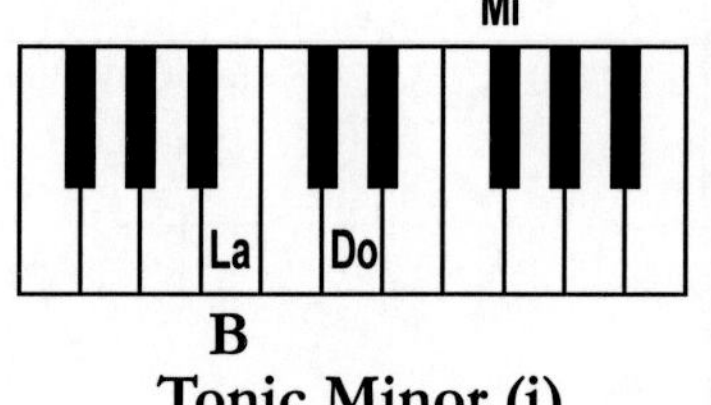

Check List

Tonic Arpeggio

Lesson		Home
________	Separated	________
________	Connected	________
________	Sing Syllables	________

Melodic Cadence

Lesson		Home
________	Hand	________
________	Hand	________
________	Separated	________
________	Connected	________
________	Sing Syllables	________
________	Add LH Roots	________

Transposition

Lesson		Home
________	Folk Song	________
________	Folk Song	________
________	Solo	________
________	Solo	________

Major Tonality - When DO is G

Tonic Arpeggio

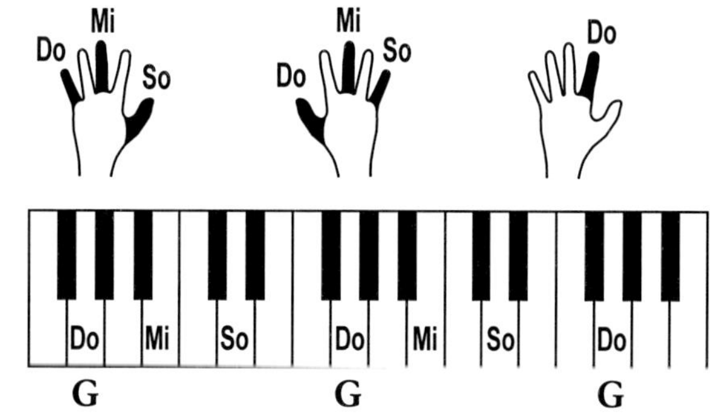

This picture is the keyboard "look" and "feel" of a G Major arpeggio: W W W

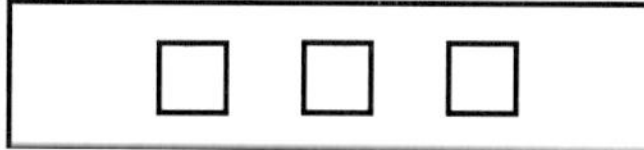

Tonic-Dominant-Tonic Melodic Cadence

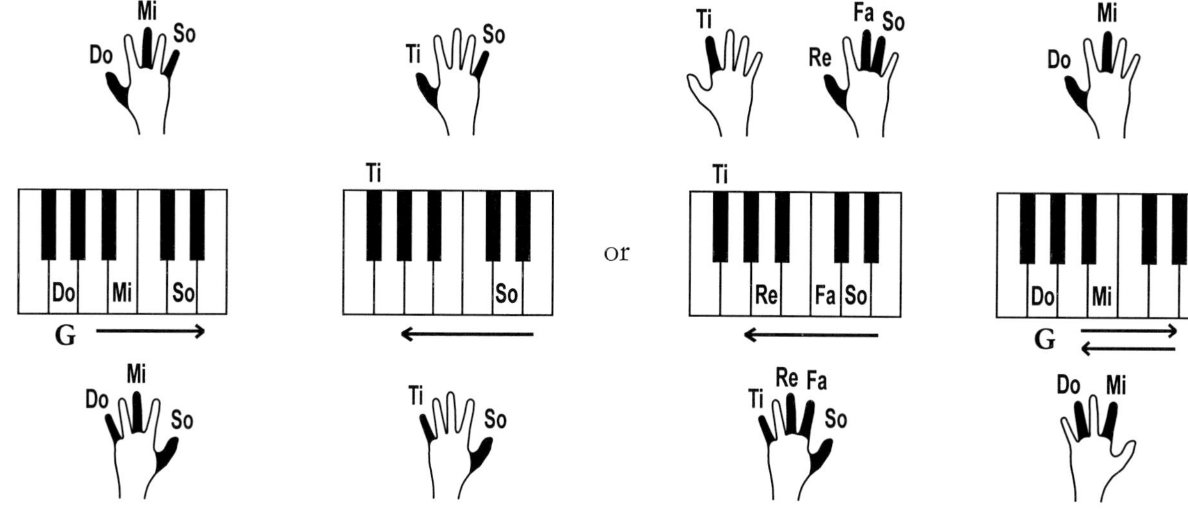

G Major Scale

DO is G

Play the scale with one finger.

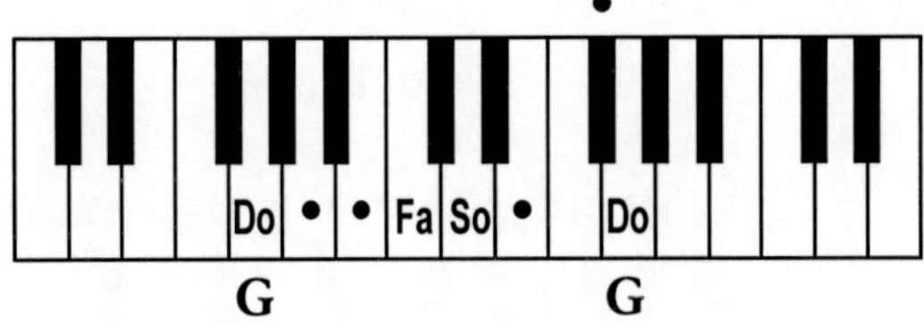

This picture is the keyboard "look" and "feel" of a G Major scale: one black key

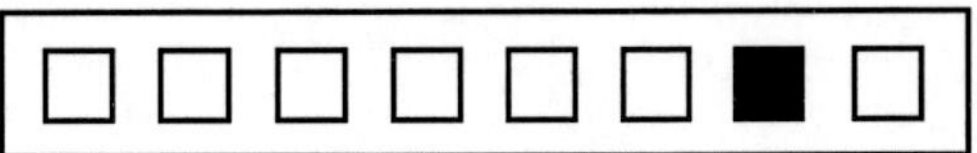

Check List

Major Scale

Lesson		Home
________	Hand	________
________	Hand	________
________	Separated	________
________	Connected	________
________	One Octave	________
________	Two Octaves	________
________	Three Octaves	________
________	Four Octaves	________

Learn the thumb crossings.

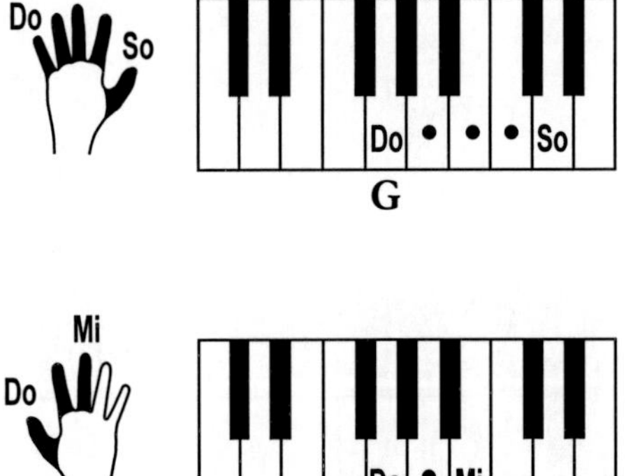

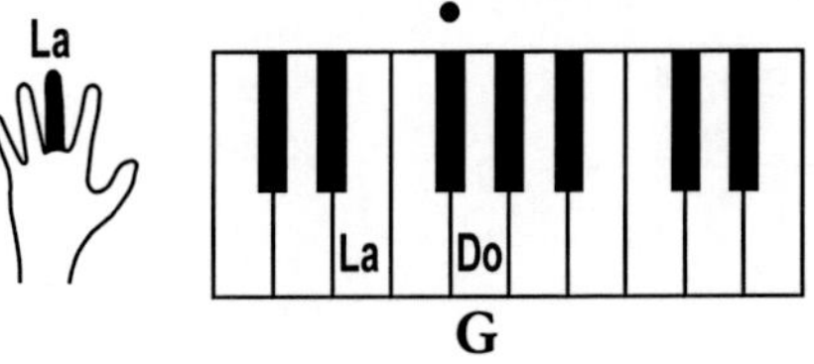

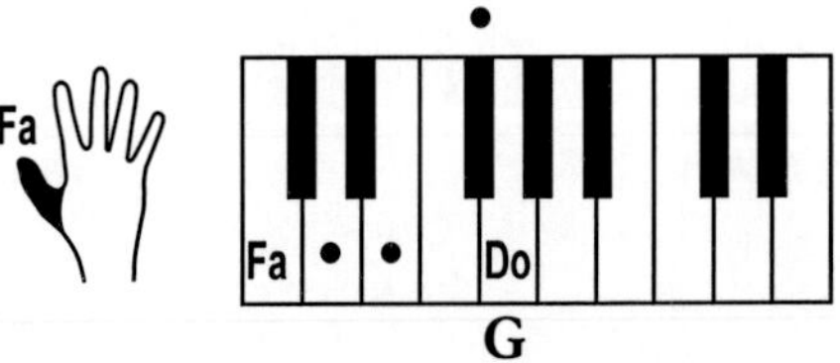

Play the scale from DO to DO.

Harmonic Minor Tonality - When LA is E

Check List

Tonic Arpeggio

Lesson		Home
________	Separated	________
________	Connected	________
________	Sing Syllables	________

Melodic Cadence

Lesson		Home
________	Hand	________
________	Hand	________
________	Separated	________
________	Connected	________
________	Sing Syllables	________
________	Add LH Roots	________

Transposition

Lesson		Home
________	Folk Song	________
________	Folk Song	________
________	Solo	________
________	Solo	________

Tonic Arpeggio

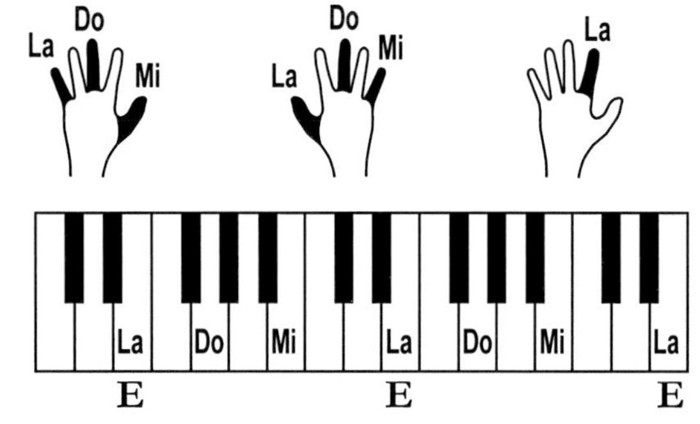

This picture is the keyboard "look" and "feel" of an E Minor arpeggio: W W W

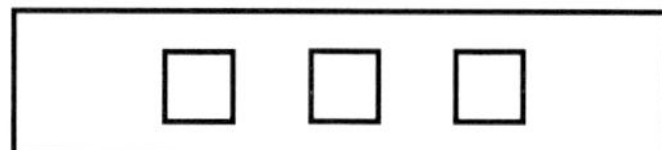

Tonic-Dominant-Tonic Melodic Cadence

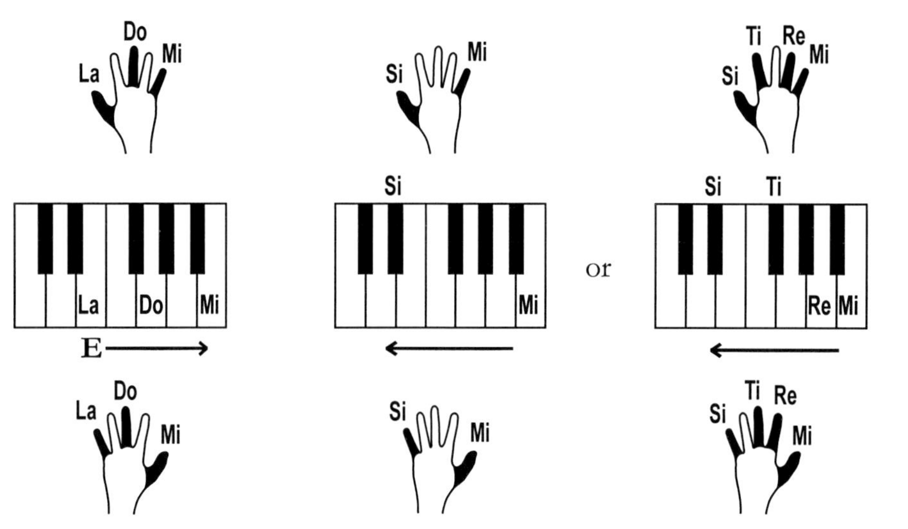

Tonic Minor (i) — Dominant Harmonic Minor (V) — Tonic Minor (i)

Tonic - Dominant - Tonic Arpeggios
When DO is G then LA is E

Check List		
Major Tonality		
Lesson		Home
________	Separated	________
________	Connected	________
________	Sing Syllables	________
Harmonic Minor Tonality		
Lesson		Home
________	Separated	________
________	Connected	________
________	Sing Syllables	________

When DO is G then LA is E

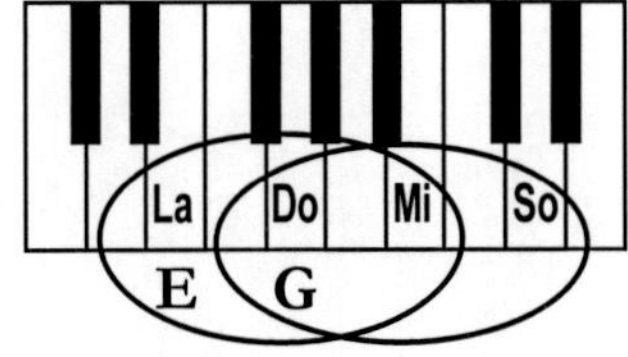

Fingers to use

Tonic-Dominant-Tonic Arpeggios

DO is G

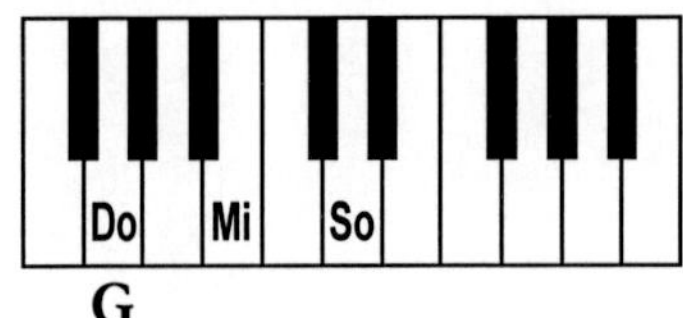

Tonic Major (I)

Ti

So Re

Dominant Major (V)

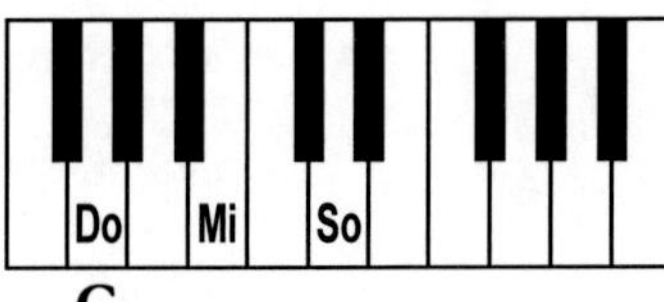

Tonic Major (I)

LA is E

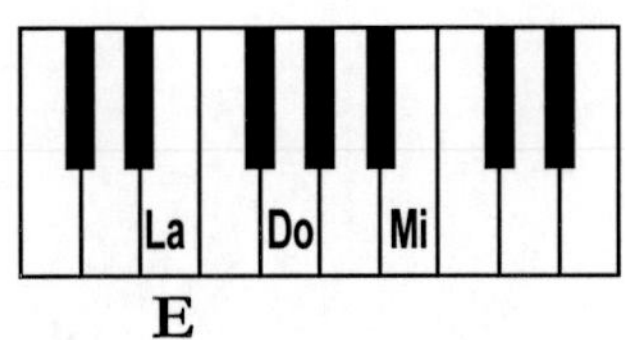

Tonic Minor (i)

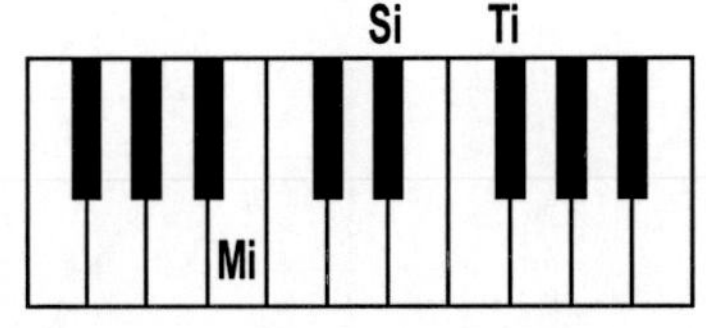

Dominant Harmonic Minor (V)

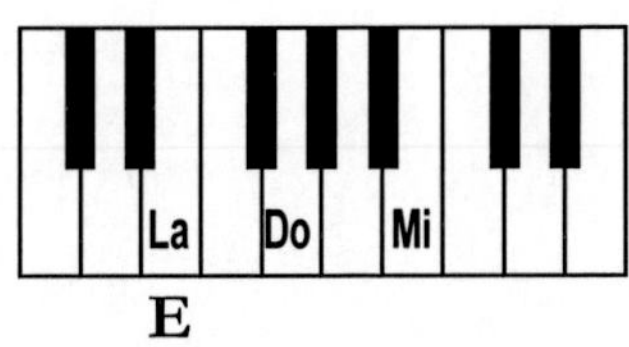

Tonic Minor (i)

Tonic - Subdominant - Tonic
When DO is G

Check List

Melodic Cadence

Lesson		Home
________	Hand	________
________	Hand	________
________	Separated	________
________	Connected	________
________	Sing Syllables	________
________	Play I-IV-V-I	________
________	Add LH Roots	________

Arpeggios

Lesson		Home
________	Separated	________
________	Connected	________
________	Sing Syllables	________
________	Play I-IV-V-I	________

Melodic Cadence

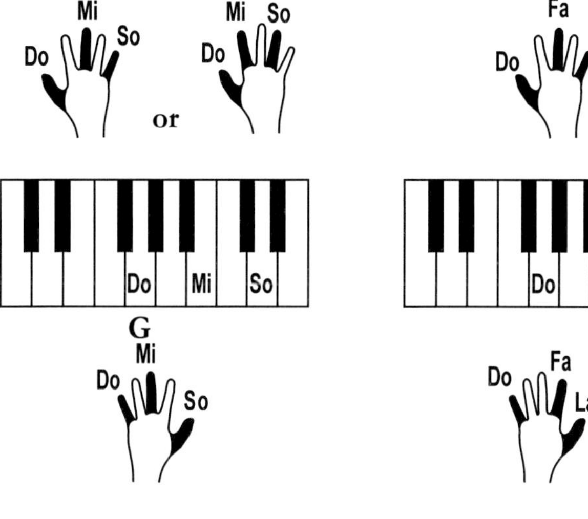

Tonic Major (I)

Subdominant Major (IV)

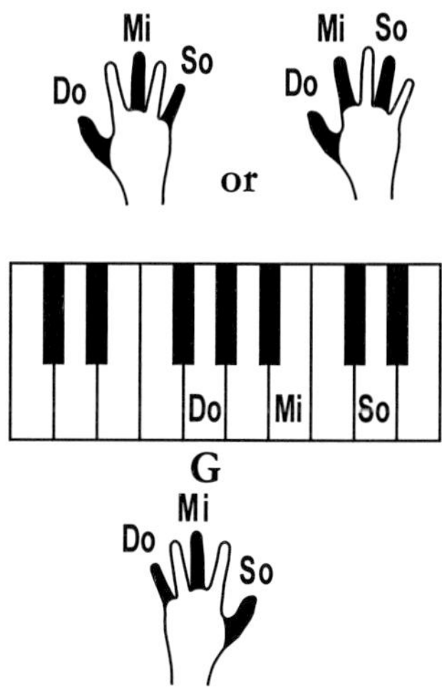

Tonic Major (I)

Arpeggios

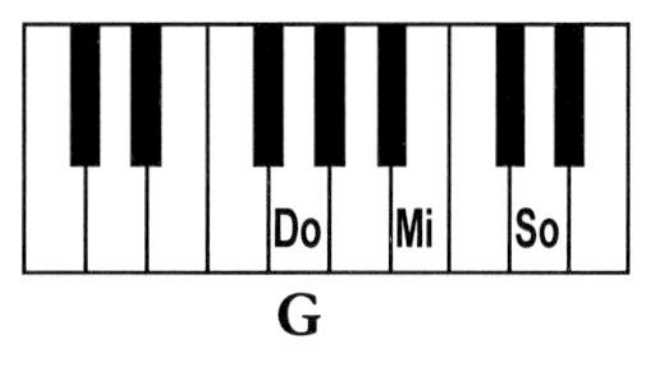

Tonic Major (I)

Fingers to Use

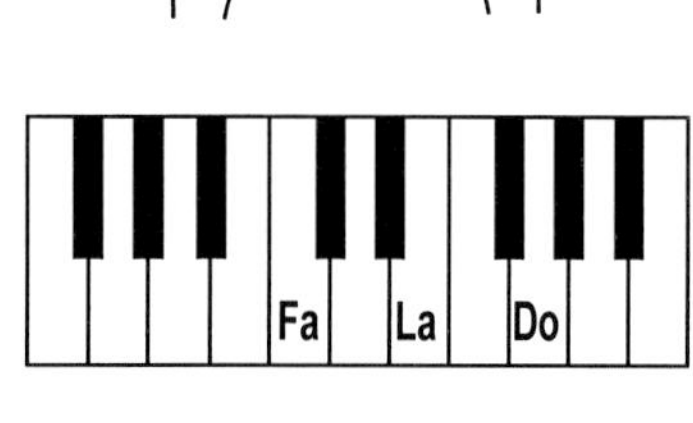

Subdominant Major (IV)

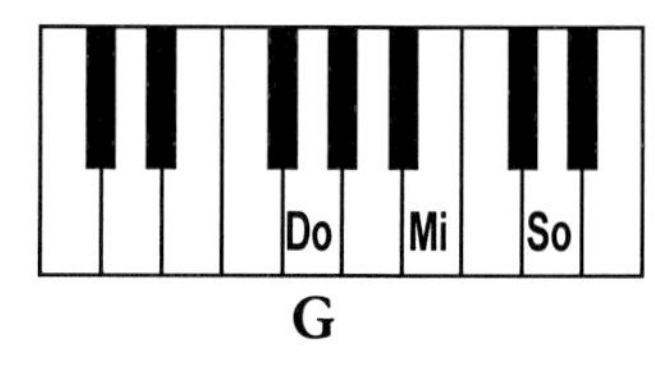

Tonic Major (I)

Tonic - Subdominant - Tonic
When LA is E

Check List

Melodic Cadence

Lesson		Home
________	Hand	________
________	Hand	________
________	Separated	________
________	Connected	________
________	Sing Syllables	________
________	Play i-iv-V-i	________
________	Add LH Roots	________

Arpeggios

Lesson		Home
________	Separated	________
________	Connected	________
________	Sing Syllables	________
________	Play i-iv-V-i	________

Melodic Cadence

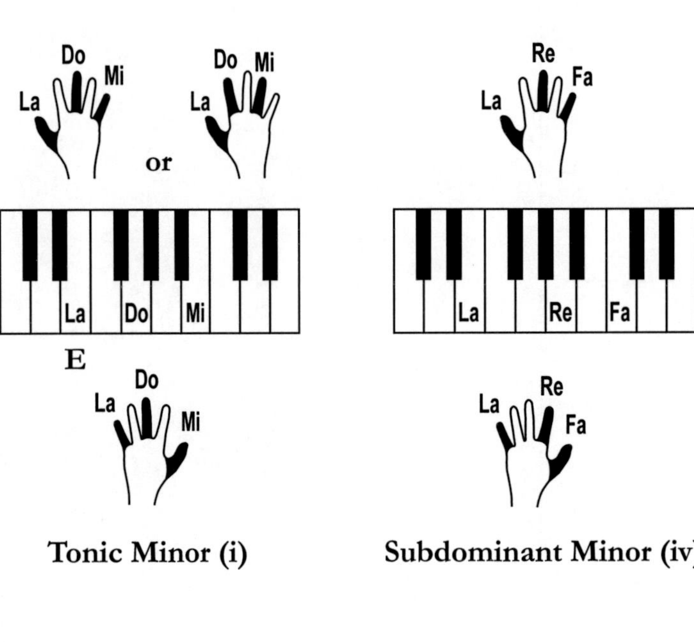

Tonic Minor (i)

Subdominant Minor (iv)

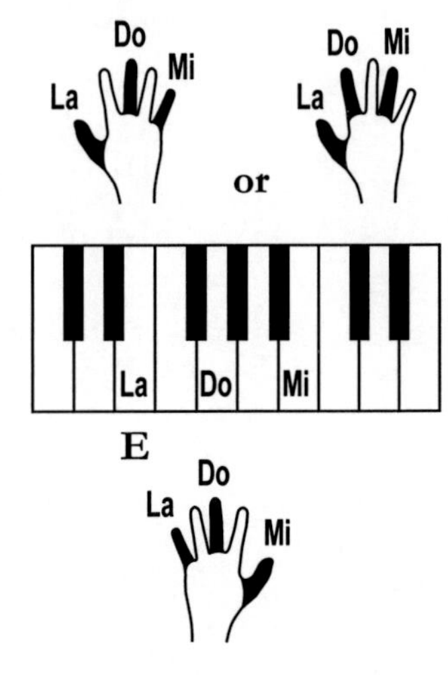

Tonic Minor (i)

Arpeggios

Fingers to Use

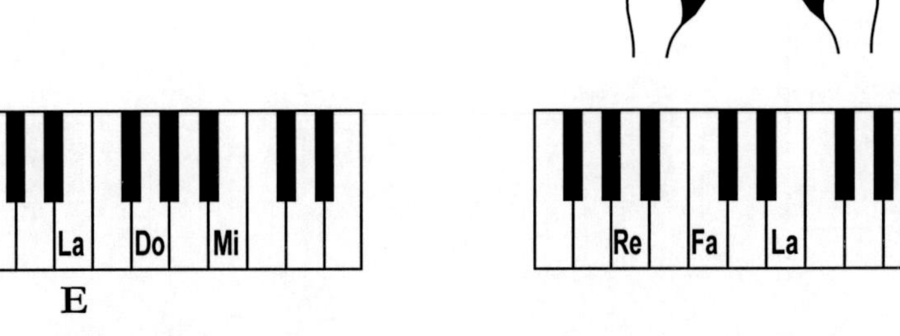

Tonic Minor (i)

Subdominant Minor (iv)

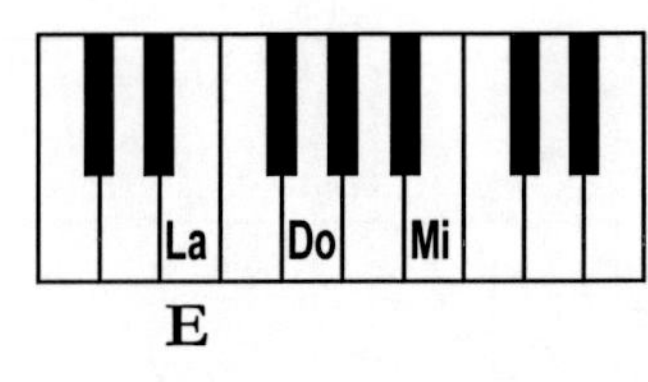

Tonic Minor (i)

Unit 13

Lesson Time Objectives

Steps for Learning New Tonalities

1. Learn and remember the resting tone for each tonality. For example, the resting tone for Dorian tonality is RE.
2. Sing the tonic triad for each tonality. For example, the tonic triad for Dorian is RE-FA-LA.
3. Learn the primary triads for each tonality.
4. Learn the melodic cadence for each tonality. The melodic cadence includes the tonic and one or two other tones.
5. Learn the characteristic tone for each tonality. The characteristic tone is the one scale tone that makes each tonality sound different.
6. Plan to master each tonality. Study one tonality for a six-week period of time in order to become immersed in the sound of the *new* tonality.

Improvisation Practice Ideas

1. Improvise a melody in one of these *new* tonalities. Use the piano or sing a melody.
2. Change a Major melody to a *new* tonality.
3. Change a Harmonic Minor melody to a *new* tonality.
4. Add root-harmony to an improvised melody in a *new* tonality.
5. Improvise two-four phrases in different tonalities. Use the same DO signature.
6. Improvise a rhythmic, contemporary sounding melody using only the scale tones from one of the *new* tonalities in this unit.

Six Other Tonalities

Description

This unit presents six tonalities that are different from Major and Harmonic Minor. Composers before 1600 A.D. wrote in these tonalitites, as well as the Beatles, other contemporary composers and early music composers.

Different sounding melodies can be composed in these tonalities by using the characteristic tone, the melodic cadential tones, and the primary triad tones. The characteristic tone is the one scale tone that makes each tonality sound different.

The melodic cadence is the tonic and one or two other tones.

Tonalities and Resting Tones

The tonalities are listed alphabetically. However, they may be studied in any order.

- Aeolian Resting tone is LA
- Dorian Resting tone is RE
- Harm Minor Resting tone is LA
- Locrian Resting tone is TI
- Lydian Resting tone is FA
- Major Resting tone is DO
- Mixolydian Resting tone is SO
- Phrygian Resting tone is MI

Primary Triads and Characteristic Tones

- Aeolian Primary triads are: i - iv - v - VII - i (characteristic tone: SO)
- Dorian Primary triads are: i -IV - VII - i (characteristic tone: TI)
- Harm Minor Primary triads are: i - iv - V - i (characteristic tone: SI)
- Locrian Primary triads are: i° -iii - vii - i° (characteristic tone: FA)
- Lydian Primary triads are: I - II - I (characteristic tone: TI)
- Major Primary triads are: I - IV - V - I (characteristic tone: TI)
- Mixolydian Primary triads are: I - IV - v - VII - I (characteristic tone: FA)
- Phrygian Primary triads are: i - II - vii - i (characteristic tone: FA)

Check List

Melodic Cadence

Lesson		Home
________	Hand	________
________	Hand	________
________	Separated	________
________	Connected	________
________	Sing Syllables	________
________	New Keyality	________
________	New Keyality	________
________	New Keyality	________
________	Add LH Roots	________

Arpeggios

Lesson		Home
________	Separated	________
________	Connected	________
________	Sing Syllables	________
________	New Keyality	________
________	New Keyality	________
________	New Keyality	________

Aeolian Tonality – When LA is G

The resting tone for Aeolian tonality is LA.
The characteristic tone for Aeolian tonality is SO.

Melodic Cadence

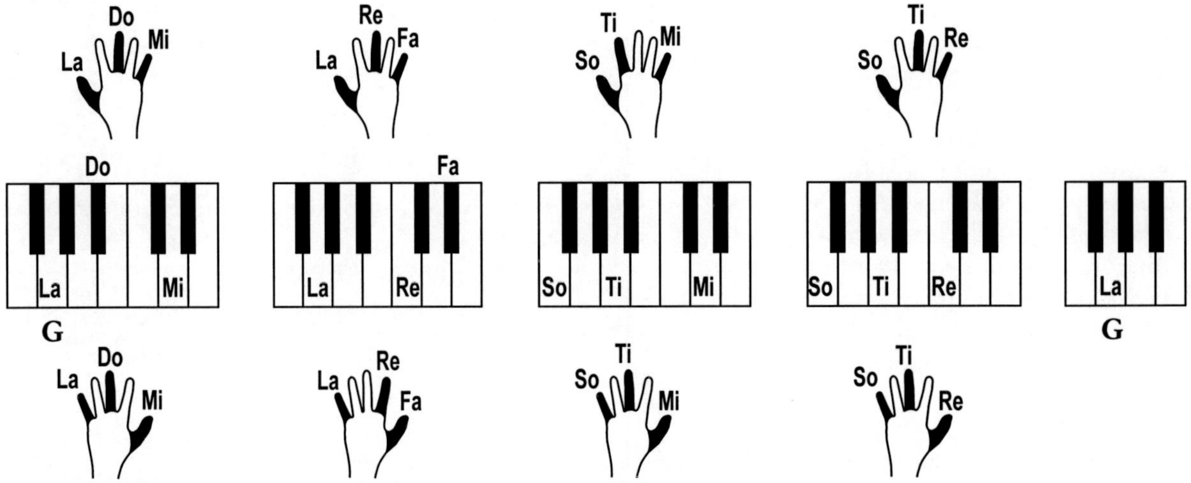

Aeolian Tonic (i) | Subdominant (iv) | Dominant (v) | Subtonic (VII) | Tonic (i)

Arpeggios

Fingers to Use

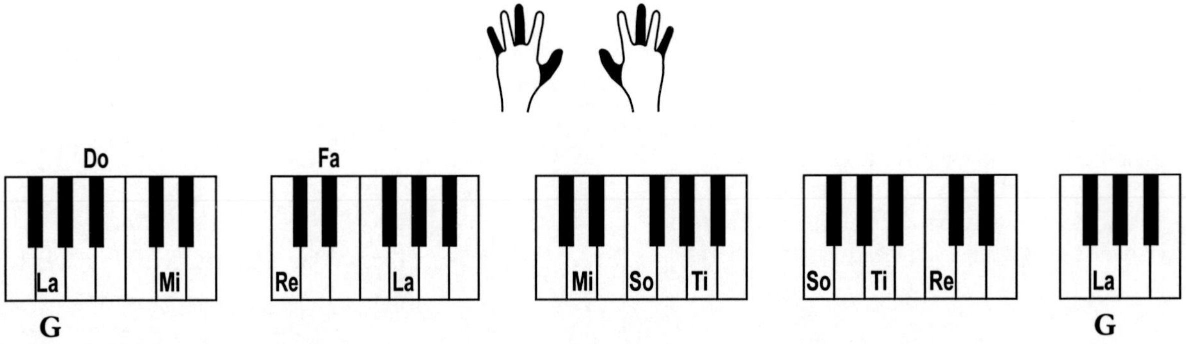

Aeolian Tonic (i) | Subdominant (iv) | Dominant (v) | Subtonic (VII) | Tonic (i)

Transpose the melodic cadence and arpeggios to other Aeolian keyalities.

Check List

Melodic Cadence

Lesson		Home
________	Hand (left)	________
________	Hand (right)	________
________	Separated	________
________	Connected	________
________	Sing Syllables	________
________	New Keyality	________
________	New Keyality	________
________	New Keyality	________
________	Add LH Roots	________

Arpeggios

Lesson		Home
________	Separated	________
________	Connected	________
________	Sing Syllables	________
________	New Keyality	________
________	New Keyality	________
________	New Keyality	________

Dorian Tonality – When RE is G

The resting tone for Dorian tonality is RE.
The characteristic tone for Dorian tonality is TI.

Melodic Cadence

Re Fa La — Re La — G — Re Fa La

Re So Ti — Re So Ti — Re So Ti

Do Mi So — Do Mi So — Do Mi So

Re Fa La — Re La — G — Re Fa La

Dorian Tonic (i) Dorian Subdominant (IV) Dorian Subtonic (VII) Dorian Tonic (i)

Arpeggios

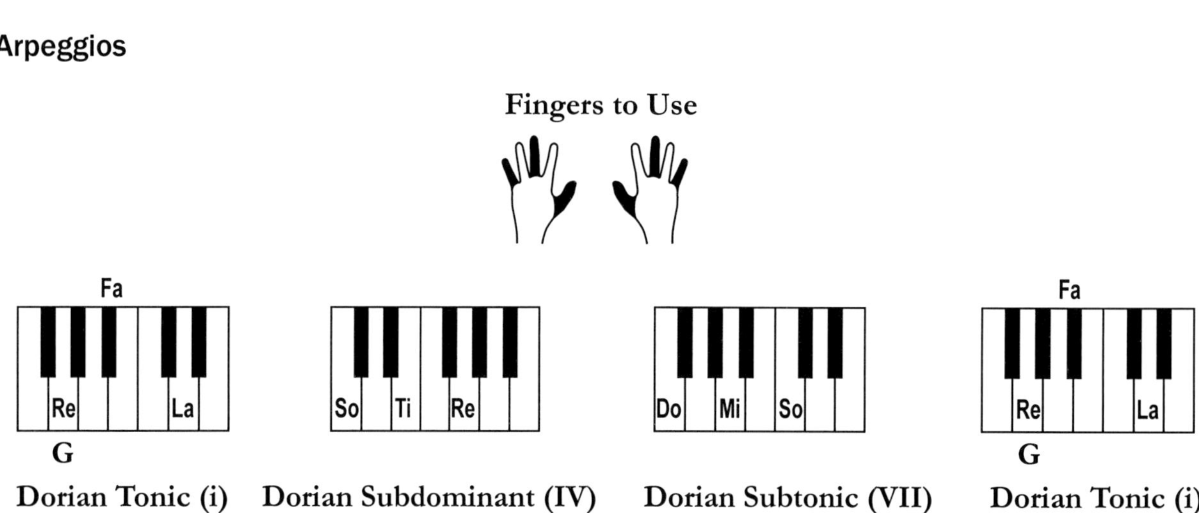

Dorian Tonic (i) Dorian Subdominant (IV) Dorian Subtonic (VII) Dorian Tonic (i)

Transpose the melodic cadence and arpeggios to other Dorian keyalities.

Locrian Tonality – When TI is G

Check List

Melodic Cadence

Lesson		Home
________	Hand	________
________	Hand	________
________	Separated	________
________	Connected	________
________	Sing Syllables	________
________	New Keyality	________
________	New Keyality	________
________	New Keyality	________
________	Add LH Roots	________

Arpeggios

Lesson		Home
________	Separated	________
________	Connected	________
________	Sing Syllables	________
________	New Keyality	________
________	New Keyality	________
________	New Keyality	________

The resting tone for Locrian tonality is TI.
The characteristic tone for Locrian tonality is FA.

Melodic Cadence

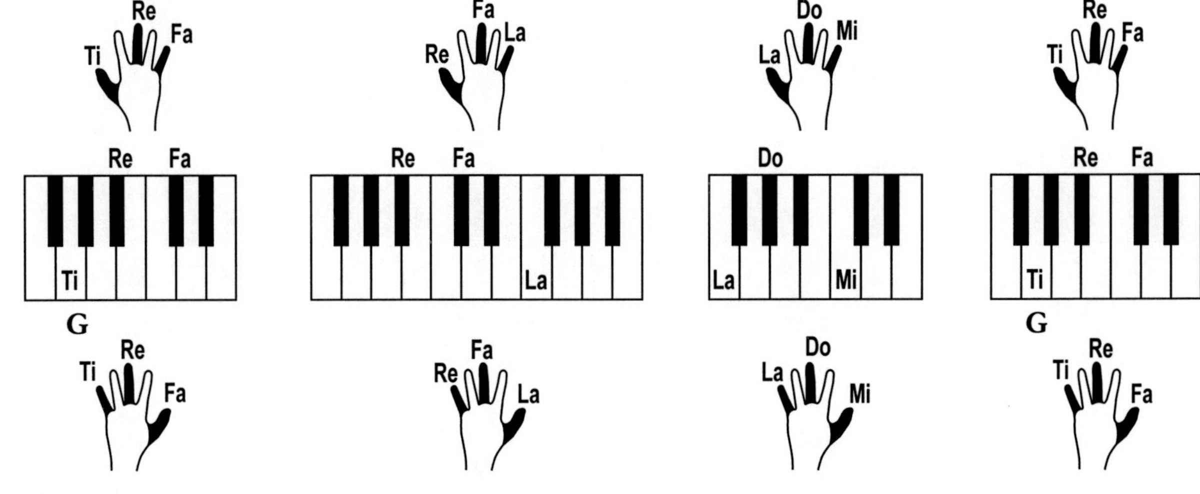

Locrian Tonic (i°) Locrian Mediant (iii) Locrian Subtonic (vii) Locrian Tonic (i°)

Arpeggios

Fingers to Use

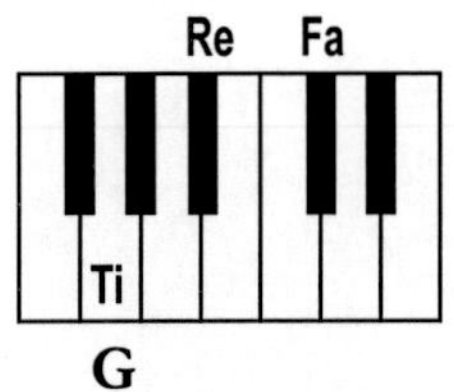

G

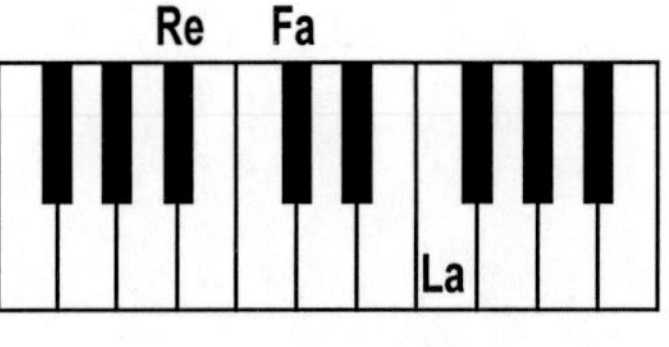

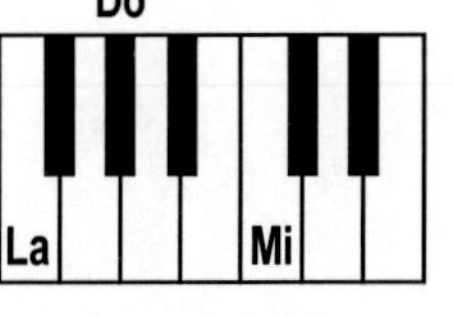

Re Fa
Ti
G

Locrian Tonic (i°) Locrian Mediant (iii) Locrian Subtonic (vii) Locrian Tonic (i°)

Transpose the melodic cadence and arpeggios to other Locrian keyalities.

Check List

Melodic Cadence

Lesson		Home
________	Hand	________
________	Hand	________
________	Separated	________
________	Connected	________
________	Sing Syllables	________
________	New Keyality	________
________	New Keyality	________
________	New Keyality	________
________	Add LH Roots	________

Arpeggios

Lesson		Home
________	Separated	________
________	Connected	________
________	Sing Syllables	________
________	New Keyality	________
________	New Keyality	________
________	New Keyality	________

Lydian Tonality – When FA is G

The resting tone for Lydian tonality is FA.
The characteristic tone for Lydian tonality is TI.

Melodic Cadence

La Do Fa | Ti Re So | La Do Fa

Ti

Fa La Do | So Re | Fa La Do

G | | G

La Fa Do | Ti So Re | La Fa Do

Lydian Tonic (I) | Lydian Supertonic (II) | Lydian Tonic (I)

Arpeggios

Fingers to Use

Ti

Fa La Do | So Re | Fa La Do

G | | G

Lydian Tonic (I) | Lydian Supertonic (II) | Lydian Tonic (I)

Transpose the melodic cadence and arpeggios to other Lydian keyalities.

Check List

Melodic Cadence

Lesson		Home
________	Hand (left)	________
________	Hand (right)	________
________	Separated	________
________	Connected	________
________	Sing Syllables	________
________	New Keyality	________
________	New Keyality	________
________	New Keyality	________
________	Add LH Roots	________

Arpeggios

Lesson		Home
________	Separated	________
________	Connected	________
________	Sing Syllables	________
________	New Keyality	________
________	New Keyality	________
________	New Keyality	________

Mixolydian Tonality – When SO is G

The resting tone for Mixolydian tonality is SO.
The characteristic tone for Mixolydian tonality is FA.

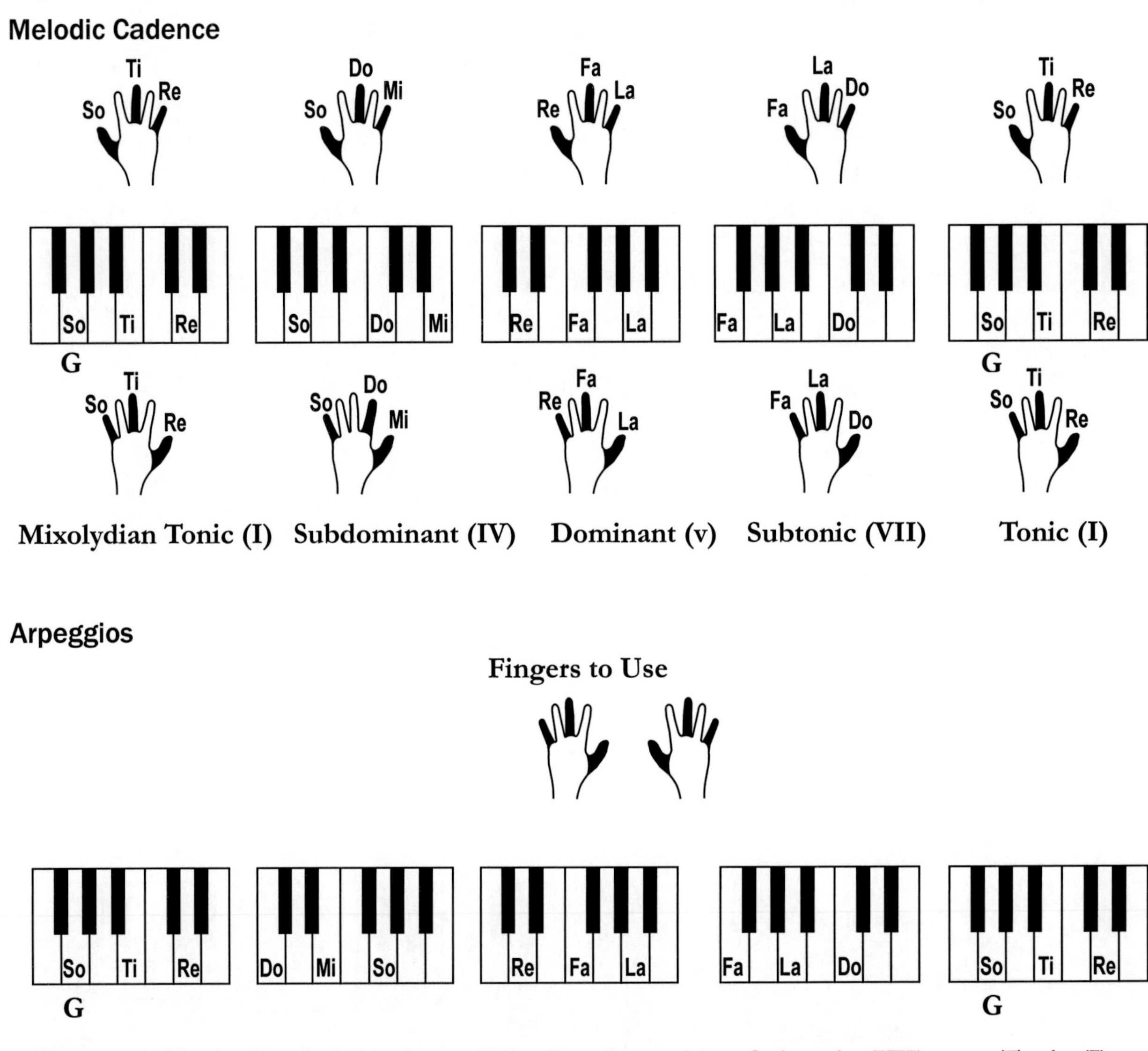

Transpose the melodic cadence and arpeggios to other Mixolydian keyalities.

Phrygian Tonality – When MI is G

Check List

Melodic Cadence

Lesson		Home
________	Hand (left)	________
________	Hand (right)	________
________	Separated	________
________	Connected	________
________	Sing Syllables	________
________	New Keyality	________
________	New Keyality	________
________	New Keyality	________
________	Add LH Roots	________

Arpeggios

Lesson		Home
________	Separated	________
________	Connected	________
________	Sing Syllables	________
________	New Keyality	________
________	New Keyality	________
________	New Keyality	________

The resting tone for Phrygian tonality is MI.
The characteristic tone for Phrygian tonality is FA.

Melodic Cadence

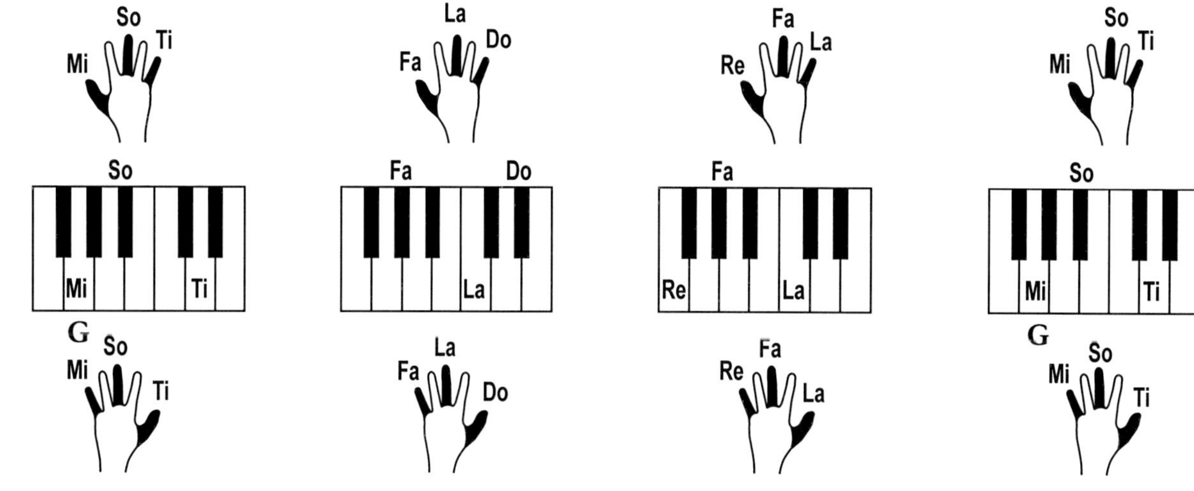

Phrygian Tonic (i) — Phrygian Supertonic (II) — Phrygian Subtonic (vii) — Phrygian Tonic (i)

Arpeggios

Fingers to Use

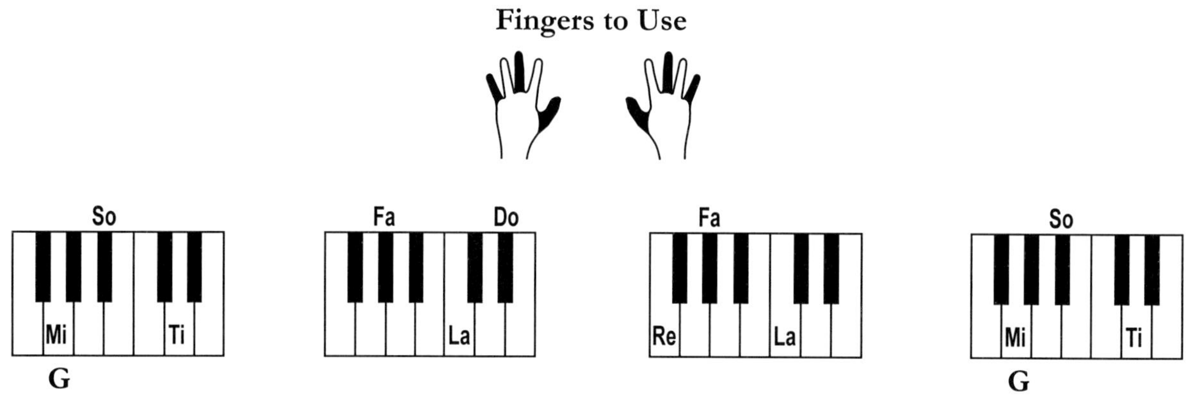

Phrygian Tonic (i) — Phrygian Supertonic (II) — Phrygian Subtonic (vii) — Phrygian Tonic (i)

Transpose the melodic cadence and arpeggios to other Phrygian keyalities.

Check List

Harmonic Minor Scale

Lesson		Home
________	Hand	________
________	Hand	________
________	Separated	________
________	Connected	________
________	Sing Syllables	________
________	New Keyality	________
________	New Keyality	________
________	New Keyality	________

Harmonic Minor Scale

About the Scale

The resting tone for Harmonic Minor tonality is LA.

To create the sound of Harmonic Minor, the dominant chord is changed to sound major by raising SO to SI.

To play a Harmonic Minor scale, use the same relative Major scale tones from LA to LA but raise SO to SI.

When G is DO then E is LA

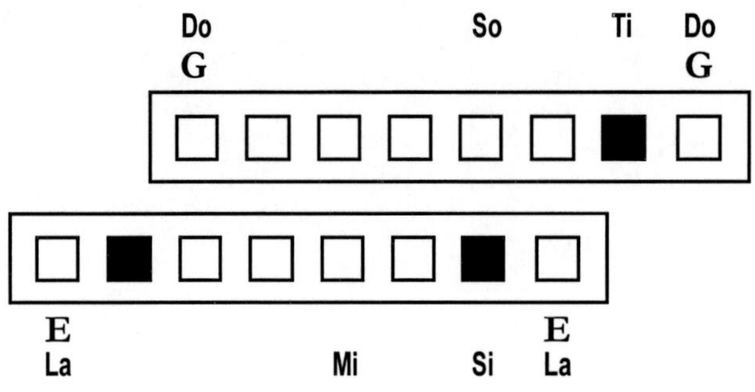

Cadences for Eight Tonalities When F is DO

Check List

Melodic Cadence

Lesson		Home
______	Hand	______
______	Hand	______
______	Separated	______
______	Connected	______
______	Sing Syllables	______
______	New Keyality	______
______	New Keyality	______
______	New Keyality	______

Arpeggios

Lesson		Home
______	Separated	______
______	Connected	______
______	Sing Syllables	______
______	New Keyality	______
______	New Keyality	______
______	New Keyality	______

Aeolian Tonality — D is LA

VII i iv v i

So La Re Mi La

D D

Dorian Tonality — G is RE

VII i IV i

Do Re So Re

G G

Harmonic Minor Tonality — D is LA

i iv V i

La Re Mi La

D D

Locrian Tonality — E is TI

vii i° iii i°

La Ti Re Ti

E E

Lydian Tonality — B♭ is FA

I II I

Fa So Fa

B♭ B♭

Major Tonality (Ionian) — F is DO

I IV V I

Do Fa So Do

F F

Mixolydian Tonality — C is SO

VII I IV v I

Fa So Do Re So

C C

Phrygian Tonality — A is MI

vii i II i

Re Mi Fa Mi

A A

Tranposition and Modulation Ideas

Check List

Transposition

Lesson		Home
________	**Hand**	________
________	**Hand**	________
________	**Chromatic**	________
________	**Whole Step**	________
________	**Circle of V**	________
________	**New Keyality**	________
________	**New Keyality**	________
________	**New Keyality**	________
________	**New Keyality**	________
________	**New Keyality**	________
________	**New Keyality**	________
________	**New Keyality**	________
________	**New Keyality**	________
________	**New Keyality**	________
________	**New Keyality**	________
________	**New Keyality**	________

Transpose Chromatically

1. Student (S) plays a song.
2. S imagines that DO is the *new* TI.
3. S plays "DO-MI-SO" in the *new* keyality.
4. S plays the song in the *new* keyality.

Transpose up a Whole Step

1. Student (S) plays a song.
2. S imagines that La is the *new* SO.
3. S plays "SO-MI-DO" in the *new* keyality.
4. S plays the song in the *new* keyality.

Transpose Around the Major Circle of Dominants

1. Student (S) plays a song that begins on SO and ends on DO. For example, "Old Woman" and "Handkerchief Dance."
2. S imagines that DO is the *new* SO.
3. S plays "SO-MI-DO" in the *new* keyality.
4. S plays the song in the *new* keyality.

Transpose a Major Song that Begins on MI and Ends on DO

1. Student (S) plays a song that begins on MI and ends on DO. "Hot Cross Buns" is an example.
2. S imagines that DO is the *new* MI.
3. S plays "MI-SO-DO" in the *new* keyality.
4. S plays the song in the *new* keyality. How many times can this melody be transposed before returning to the starting keyality?

Minor Tonality Songs

Use the above transposition examples for songs in Minor tonality. Use the same steps, but substitute LA-DO-MI for DO-MI-SO and SI for TI.

Practice the Following

Lesson	Home	
________	________	In Major tonality, play DO and the *new* chromatic DO-SO-DO, each hand alone. Play in many keyalities.
________	________	In Minor tonality, play LA and the *new* chromatic LA-MI-LA, each hand alone. Play in many keyalities.
________	________	In Major tonality, play DO-LA. Imagine LA as the *new* SO. Play the *new* SO-MI-DO, each hand alone. Play in many keyalities.
________	________	In Minor tonality, play LA-FA. Imagine FA as the *new* MI. Play the *new* MI-DO-LA. Play in many keyalities.
________	________	In Major tonality, play DO. Imagine DO as the *new* SO. Play the *new* SO-MI-DO. Play in many keyalities.
________	________	In Minor tonality, play LA. Imagine LA as the *new* MI. Play the *new* MI-DO-LA. Play in many keyalities.
________	________	In Major tonality, play DO. Imagine DO as the *new* MI. Play the *new* MI-SO-DO. Play in many keyalities.
________	________	In Minor tonality, play LA. Imagine LA as the *new* DO. Then play the *new* DO-LA-DO. Play in many keyalities.